36th (Texas) Division

Divisional Components of the U.S. Army
1917-2004

© Timothy Aumiller 2005

ISBN 0972029656

The purpose of writing the book is to honor the veterans who served in the divisions of the United States Army from World War I to 2004.

Many vets want to know what happened to their outfits after so many years have passed. And the descendents of vets might also like to learn more about their ancestor's unit.

It was talking to my father and other World War II vets that gave me the idea for this book.

I would particularly like to honor my father, T/4 Kermit A. Aumiller, and my uncle, PFC George D. Aumiller. If it were not for these "ordinary" persons and millions of others who served, we would not have the extraordinary country that today is the United States of America.

Published for Orbat.com by

Tiger Lily Publication LLC

2005

40th Infantry Division ("Sunrise"), California

29th Infantry Division

This division is associated with the States of Maryland and Virginia, which fought on opposite sides in the War Between the States. The division embodies units from both the Confederate and Union Armies, and symbolizes reconciliation and the unity of the United States. – the Blue and the Gray.

References

Army Lineage Series, Center for Military History.
Divisional Websites,
Divisional Association Websites
Other Public Domain materials and Websites

75th Infantry Division

The 42nd Division stretches like a Rainbow from one end of America to the other."
General Douglas Macarthur. The division recruited from 27 states.

Contents

82nd Airborne Division "All American"

The first US division to be recruited on a national basis.

1917

1st Division-Active Component-Big Red One-1917

1st 2nd Infantry Brigade
16th 18th 26th 28th Infantry Regiments

1st Field Artillery Brigade
5th 6th 7th Field Artillery Regiments

1st 2nd 3rd Machine Gun Battalions

1st Trench Mortar Battery
1st Engineer Regiment
1st Field Signal Battalion
1st Division Train Headquarters & Military Police
1st Supply Train
1st Ammunition Train
1st Engineer Train
1st Sanitary Train
2nd 3rd 12th 13th Ambulance Companies & Field Hospitals

2nd Division-Active Component-Indianhead-1917

3rd 4th Infantry Brigades
9th 23rd Infantry Regiments
5th 6th Marine Regiments

2nd Field Artillery Brigade
12th 15th 17th Field Artillery Regiments

4th 5th 6th Machine Gun Battalions

2nd Trench Mortar Battery
2nd Engineer Regiment
2nd Field Signal Battalion
2nd Division Train Headquarters & Military Police
2nd Supply Train
2nd Ammunition Train
2nd Engineer Train

2nd Sanitary Train
1st 15th 16th 23rd Ambulance Companies & Field Hospitals

3rd Division-Active Component-Marne-1917

5th 6th Infantry Brigades
4th 7th 30th 38th Infantry Regiments

3rd Field Artillery Brigade
10th 18th 76th Field Artillery Regiments

7th 8th 9th Machine Gun Battalions

3rd Trench Mortar Battery
6th Engineer Regiment
5th Field Signal Battalion
3rd Division Train Headquarters & Military Police
3rd Supply Train
3rd Ammunition Train
6th Engineer Train
3rd Sanitary Train
5th 7th 26th 27th Ambulance Companies & Field Hospitals

4th Division-Active Component-Ivy-1917

7th 8th Infantry Brigades
39th 47th 58th 59th Infantry Regiments

4th Field Artillery Brigade
13th 15th 77th Field Artillery Regiments

10th 11th 12th Machine Gun Battalions

4th Trench Mortar Battery
4th Engineer Regiment
4th Field Signal Battalion
4th Division Train Headquarters & Military Police
4th Supply Train
4th Ammunition rain
4th Sanitary Train
19th 21st 28th 33rd Ambulance Companies & Field Hospitals

6th Division-Active Component-Red Star-1917

11th 12th Infantry Brigades
51st 52nd 53rd 54th Infantry Regiments

6th Field Artillery Brigade
3rd 11th 78th Field Artillery Regiments

16th 17th 18th Machine Gun Battalions

6th Trench Mortar Battery
318th Engineer Regiment
6th Field Signal Battalion
6th Division Train Headquarters & Military Police
6th Supply Train
6th Ammunition Train
318th Engineer Train
6th Sanitary Train
20th 37th 38th 40th Ambulance Companies & Field Hospitals

7th Division-Active Component-Bayonet-1917

13th 14th Infantry Brigades
13th 34th 56th 64th Infantry Regiments

7th Field Artillery Brigade
8th 79th 80th Field Artillery Regiments

19th 20th 21st Machine Gun Battalions

7th Trench Mortar Battery
5th Engineer Regiment
10th Field Signal Battalion
7th Division Train Headquarters & Military Police
7th Supply Train
7th Ammunition Train
5th Engineer Train
7th Sanitary Train
12th 34th 35th 36th Ambulance Companies & Field Hospitals

8th Division-Active Component-Pathfinders-1917

15th 16th Infantry Brigades
8th 12th 13th 62nd Infantry Regiments

8th Field Artillery Brigade
2nd 81st 83rd Field Artillery Regiments

22nd 23rd 24th Machine Gun Battalions

8th Trench Mortar Battery
319th Engineer Regiment
320th Field Signal Battalion
8th Division Train Headquarters & Military Police
8th Supply Train
8th Ammunition Train
320th Engineer Train
8th Sanitary Train
11th 31st 32nd 43rd Ambulance Companies & Field Hospitals

9th Division-Active Component-Varsity-1917

17th 18th Infantry Brigades
45th 46th 67th 68th Infantry Regiments

9th Field Artillery Brigade
25th 26th 27th Field Artillery Regiments

25th 26th 27th Machine Gun Battalions

9th Trench Mortar Battery
109th Engineer Regiment
209th Field Signal Battalion
9th division Train Headquarters & Military Police
9th Supply Train
9th Ammunition Train
209th Engineer Train
9th Sanitary Train
233rd 234th 235th 236th Ambulance Companies & Field Hospitals

10th Division-Active Component-1917

19th 20th Infantry Brigades
20th 41st 69th 70th Infantry Regiments

10th Field Artillery Brigade
28th 29th 30th Field Artillery Regiments

28th 29th 30th Machine Gun Battalions

10th Trench Mortar Battery
210th Engineer Regiment
210th Field Signal Battalion
10th Division Train Headquarters & Military Police
10th Supply Train
10 Ammunition Train
210th Engineer Train
10th Sanitary Train
237th 238th 239th 240th Ambulance Companies & Field Hospitals

11th Division-Active Component-1918

21st 22nd Infantry Brigades
17th 63rd 71st 72nd Infantry Regiments

11th Field Artillery Brigade
31st 32nd 33rd Field Artillery Regiments

31st 32nd 33rd Machine Gun Battalions

11th Trench Mortar Battery
211th Engineer Regiment
211th Field Signal Battalion
11th Division Train Headquarters & Military Police
11th Supply Train
11th Ammunition Train
211th Engineer Train
11th Sanitary Train
241st 242nd 243rd 244th Ambulance Companies & Field Hospitals

12th Division-Active Component-1918

23rd 24th Infantry Brigade
36th 42nd 73rd 74th Infantry Regiments

12th Field Artillery Brigade
34th 35th 36th Field Artillery Regiments

34th 35th 36th Machine Gun Battalions

12th Trench Mortar Battery
212th Engineer Regiment
212th Field Signal Battalion
12th Division Train Headquarters & Military Police
12th Supply Train
12th Ammunition Train
212th Engineer Train
245th 246th 247th 248th Ambulance Companies & Field Hospitals

13th Division-Active Component-1918

25th 26th Infantry Brigades
1st 44th 75th 76th Infantry Regiments

13th Field Artillery Brigade
37th 38th 39th Field Artillery Regiments

37th 38th 39th Machine Gun Battalions

13th Trench Mortar Battery
213th Engineer Regiment
213th Field Signal Battalion
13th Division Train Headquarters & Military Police
13th Supply Train
13th Ammunition Train
213th Engineer Train
13th Sanitary Train
249th 250th 251st 252nd Ambulance Companies & Field Hospitals

14th Division-Active Component-1918

27th 28th Infantry Brigades
10th 40th 77th 78th Infantry Regiments

14th Field Artillery Brigade
40th 41st 42nd Field Artillery Regiments

40th 41st 42nd Machine Gun Battalions

14th Trench Mortar Battery
214th Engineer Regiment
214th Field Signal Battalion
14th Division Train Headquarters & Military Police
14th Supply Train
14th Ammunition Train
214th Engineer Train
14th Sanitary Train
253rd 254th 255th 256th Ambulance Companies & Field Hospitals

15th Division-Active Component-1918

29th 30th Infantry Brigades
43rd 57th 79th 80th Infantry Regiments

15th Field Artillery Brigade
43rd 44th 45th Field Artillery Regiments

43rd 44th 45th Machine Gun Battalions

15th Trench Mortar Battery
215th Engineer Regiment
215th Field Signal Battalion
15th Division Train Headquarters & Military Police
15th Supply Train
15th Ammunition Train
215th Engineer Train
15th Sanitary Train
257th 258th 259th 260th Ambulance Companies & Field Hospitals

16th Division-Active Component-1918

31st 32nd Infantry Brigades
21st 31st 81st 82nd Infantry Regiments

16th Field Artillery Brigade
46th 47th 48th Field Artillery Regiments

46th 47th 48th Machine Gun Battalions

16th Trench Mortar Battery
216th Engineer Regiment
216th Field Signal Battalion
16th Division Train Headquarters
16th Supply Train
16th Ammunition Train
216th Engineer Train
16th Sanitary Train
261st 262nd 263rd 264th Ambulance Companies & Field Hospitals

17th Division-Active Component-1918

33rd 34th Infantry Brigades
5th 29th 83rd 84th Infantry Regiments

17th Field Artillery Brigade
49th 50th 51st Field Artillery Regiments

49th 50th 51st Machine Gun Battalions

17th Trench Mortar Battery
217th Engineer Regiment
217th Field Signal Battalion
17th Division Train Headquarters & Military Police
17th Supply Train
17th Ammunition Train
217th Engineer Train
17th Sanitary Train
265th 266th 267th 268th Ambulance Companies & Field Hospitals

18th Division-Active Component-1918

35th 36th Infantry Brigades
19th 35th 85th 86th Infantry Regiments

18th Field Artillery Brigade
52nd 53rd 54th Field Artillery Regiments

52nd 53rd 54th Machine Gun Battalions

18th Trench Mortar Battery
218th Engineer Regiment
218th Field Signal Battalion
18th Division Train Headquarters & Military Police
18th Supply Train
18th Ammunition Train
218th Engineer Train
18th Sanitary Train
269th 270th 271st 272nd Ambulance Companies & Field Hopsitals

19th Division-Active Component-1918

37th 38th Infantry Brigades
2nd 14th 87th 88th Infantry Regiments

19th Field Artillery Brigade
55th 56th 57th Field Artillery Regiments

55th 56th 57th Machine Gun Battalions

19th Trench Mortar Battery
219th Engineer Regiment
219th Field Signal Battalion
19th Supply Train
19th Ammunition Train
219th Engineer Train
273rd 274th 275th 276th Ambulance Companies & Field Hospitals

20th Division-Active Component-1918

39th 40th Infantry Brigades
48th 50th 89th 90th Infantry Regiments

20th Field Artillery Brigade
58th 59th 60th Field Artillery Regiments

58th 59th 60th Machine Gun Battalions

20th Trench Mortar Battery
220th Engineer Regiment
220th Field Signal Battalion
20th Division Train Headquarters & Military Police
20th Supply Train
20th Ammunition Train
220th Engineer Train
20th Sanitary Train
277th 278th 279th 280th Ambulance Companies & Field Hospitals

26th Division-National Guard-Yankee-1917

51st 52nd Infantry Brigades
101st 102nd 103rd 104th Infantry Regiments

51st Field Artillery Brigade
101st 102nd 103rd Field Artillery Regiments

101st 102nd 103rd Machine Gun Battalions

101st Trench Mortar Battery
101st Engineer Regiment
101st Field Signal Battalion
101st Division Train Headquarters & Military Police
101st Supply Train
101st Ammunition Train
101st Engineer Train
101st Sanitary Train
101st 102nd 103rd 104th Ambulance Companies & Field Hospitals

27th Division-National Guard-New York-1917

53rd 54th Infantry Brigades
105th 106th 107th 108th Infantry Regiments

52nd Field Artillery Brigade
104th 105th 106th Field Artillery Regiments

104th 105th 106th Machine Gun Battalions

102nd Trench Mortar Battery
102nd Engineer Regiment
102nd Field signal Battalion
102nd Division Train Headquarters & Military Police
102nd Supply Train
102nd Ammunition Train
102nd Engineer Train
102nd Sanitary Train
105th 106th 107th 108th Ambulance Companies & Field Hospitals

28th Division-National Guard-National Guard-1917

55th 56th Infantry Brigades
109th 110th 111th 112th Infantry Regiments

53rd Field Artillery Brigade
107th 108th 109th Field Artillery Regiments

107th 108th 109th Machine Gun Battalions

103rd Trench Mortar Battery
103rd Engineer Regiment
103rd Field Signal Battalion
103rd Division Train Headquarters & Military Police
103rd Supply Train
103rd Ammunition Train
103rd Engineer Train
103rd Sanitary Train
109th 110th 111th 112th Ambulance Companies & Field Hospitals

29th Division-National Guard-Keystone-1917

57th 58th Infantry Brigades
113th 114th 115th 116th Infantry Regiments

54th Field Artillery Brigade
110th 111th 112th Field Artillery Regiments

110th 111th 112th Machine Gun Battalions

104th Trench Mortar Battery
104th Engineer Regiment
104th Field Signal Battalion
104th Division Train Headquarters & Military Police
104th Supply Train
104th Ammunition Train
104th Engineer Train
104th Sanitary Train
113th 114th 115th 116th Ambulance Companies & Field Hospitals

30th Division-National Guard-Old Hickory-1917

59th 60th Infantry Brigades
117th 118th 119th 120th Infantry Regiments

55th Field Artillery Brigade
113th 114th 115th Field Artillery Regiments

113th 114th 115th Machine Gun Battalions

105th Trench Mortar Battery
105th Engineer Regiment
105th Field Signal Battalion
105th Division Train Headquarters & Military Police
105th Supply Train
105th Ammunition Train
105th Engineer Train
105th Sanitary Train
117th 118th 119th 120th Ambulance Companies & Field Hospitals

31st Division-National Guard-Dixie-1917

61st 62nd Infantry Brigades
121st 122nd 123rd 124th Infantry Regiments

56th Field Artillery Brigade
116th 117th 118th Field Artillery Regiments

116th 117th 118th Machine Gun Battalions

106th Trench Mortar Battery
106th Engineer Regiment
106th Field Signal Battalion
106th Division Train Headquarters & Military Police
106th Supply Train
106th Ammunition Train
106th Engineer Train
106th Sanitary Train
121st 122nd 123rd 124th Ambulance Companies & Field Hospitals

32nd Division-National Guard-Red Arrow-1917

63rd 64th Infantry Brigades
125th 126th 127th 128th Infantry Regiments

57th Field Artillery Brigade
119th 120th 121st Field Artillery Regiments

119th 120th 121st Machine Gun Battalions

107th Trench Mortar Battery
107th Engineer Regiment
107th Field Signal Battalion
107th Division Train Headquarters & Military Police
107th Supply Train
107th Ammunition Train
107th Engineer Train
107th Sanitary Train
125th 126th 127th 128th Ambulance Companies & Field Hospitals

33rd Division-National Guard-Prairie-1917

65th 66th Infantry Brigades
129th 130th 131st 132nd Infantry Regiments

58th Field Artillery Brigade
122nd 123rd 124th Field Artillery Regiments

122nd 123rd 124th Machine Gun Battalions

108th Trench Mortar Battery
108th Engineer Regiment
108th Field signal Battalion
108th Division Train Headquarters & Military Police
108th Supply Train
108th Ammunition Train
108th Engineer Train
108th Sanitary Train
129th 130th 131st 132nd Ambulance Companies & Field Hospitals

34th Division-National Guard-Red Bull-1917

67th 68th Infantry Brigades
133rd 134th 135th 136th Infantry Regiments

59th Field Artillery Brigade
125th 126th 127th Field Artillery Regiments

125th 126th 127th Machine Gun Battalions

109th Trench Mortar Battery
109th Engineer Regiment
109th Field Signal Battalion
109th Division Train Headquarters & Military Police
109th Supply Train
109th Ammunition Train
109th Engineer Train
109th Sanitary Train
133rd 134th 135th 136th Ambulance Companies & Field Hospitals

35th Division-National Guard-Santa Fe-1917

69th 70th Infantry Brigades
137th 138th 139th 140th Infantry Regiments

60th Field Artillery Brigade
128th 129th 130th Field Artillery Regiments

128th 129th 130th Machine Gun Battalions

110th Trench Mortar Battery
110th Engineer Regiment
110th Field Signal Battalion
110th Division Train Headquarters & Military Police
110th Supply Train
110th Ammunition Train
110th Engineer Train
110th Sanitary Train
137th 138th 139th 140th Ambulance & Field Hospitals

36th Division-National Guard-Texas-1917

71st 72nd Infantry Brigades
141st 142nd 143rd 144th Infantry Regiments

61st Field Artillery Brigade
131st 132nd 133rd Field Artillery Regiments

131st 132nd 133rd Machine Gun Battalions

111th Trench Mortar Battery
111th Engineer Regiment
111th Field Signal Battalion
111th Division Train Headquarters & Military Police
111th Supply Train
111th Ammunition Train
111th Engineer Train
111th Sanitary Train
141st 142nd 143rd 144th Ambulance Companies & Field Hospitals

37th Division-National Guard-Buckeye-1917

73rd 74th Infantry Brigades
145th 146th 147th 148th Infantry Regiments

62nd Field Artillery Brigade
134th 135th 136th Field Artillery Regiments

134th 135th 136th Machine Gun Battalions

112th Trench Mortar Battery
112th Engineer Battalion
112th Field Signal Battalion
112th Division Train Headquarters & Military Police
112th Supply Train
112th Ammunition Train
112th Engineer Train
112th Sanitary Train
145th 146th 147th 148th Ambulance Companies & Field Hospitals

38th Division-National Guard-Cyclone-1917

75th 76th Infantry Brigades
149th 150th 151st 152nd Infantry Regiments

63rd Field Artillery Brigade
137th 138th 139th Field Artillery Regiments

137th 138th 139th Machine Gun Battalions

113th Trench Mortar Battery
113th Engineer Regiment
113th Field Signal Battalion
113th Division Train Headquarters & Military Police
113th Supply Train
113th Ammunition Train
113th Engineer Train
149th 150th 151st 152nd Ambulance Companies & Field Hospitals

39th Division-National Guard-Delta-1917

77th 78th Infantry Brigades
153rd 154th 155th 156th Infantry Regiments

64th Field Artillery Brigade
140th 141st 142nd Field Artillery Regiments

140th 141st 142nd Machine Gun Battalions

114th Trench Mortar Battery
114th Engineer Regiment
114th Field Signal Battalion
114th Division Train Headquarters & Military Police
114th Supply Train
114th Ammunition Train
114th Engineer Train
114th Sanitary Train
153rd 154th 155th 156th Ambulance Companies & Field Hospitals

40th Division-National Guard-Sunrise-1917

79th 80th Infantry Brigades
157th 158th 159th 160th Infantry Regiments

65th Field Artillery Brigade
143rd 144th 145th Field Artillery Regiments

143rd 144th 145th Machine Gun Battalions

115th Trench Mortar Battery
115th Engineer Regiment
115th Field Signal Battalion
115th Division Train Headquarters & Military Police
115th Supply Train
115th Ammunition Train
115th Engineer Train
115th Sanitary Train
157th 158th 159th 160th Ambulance Companies & Field Hospitals

41st Division-National Guard-Sunset-1917

81st 82nd Infantry Brigades
161st 162nd 163rd 164th Infantry Regiments

66th Field Artillery Brigade
146th 147th 148th Field Artillery Regiments

146th 147th 148th Machine Gun Battalions

116th Trench Mortar Battery
116th Engineer Regiment
116th Field Signal Battalion
116th Division Train Headquarters & Military Police
116th Supply Train
116th Ammunition Train
116th Sanitary Train
161st 162nd 163rd 164th Ambulance Companies & Field Hospitals

42nd Division-National Guard-Rainbow-1917

83rd 84th Infantry Brigades
165th 166th 167th 168th Infantry Regiments

67th Field Artillery Brigade
149th 150th 151st Field Artillery Regiments

149th 150th 151st Machine Gun Battalions

117th Trench Mortar Battery
117th Engineer Regiment
117th Field Signal Battalion
117th Division Train Headquarters & Military Police
117th Supply Train
117th Ammunition Train
117th Engineer Train
117th Sanitary Train
165th 166th 167th 168th Ambulance Companies & Field Hospitals

76th Division-National Army-Onaway-1917

151st 152nd Infantry Brigades
301st 302nd 303rd 304th Infantry Regiments

151st Field Artillery Brigade
301st 302nd 303rd Field Artillery Regiments

301st 302nd 303rd Machine Gun Battalions

301st Trench Mortar Battery
301st Engineer Regiment
301st Field Signal Battalion
301st Division Train Headquarters & Military Police
301st Supply Train
301st Ammunition Train
301st Engineer Train
301st Sanitary Train
301st 302nd 303rd 304th Ambulance Companies & Field Hospitals

77th Division-National Army-Statue of Libert1-1917

153rd 154th Infantry Brigades
305th 306th 307th 308th Infantry Regiments

152nd Field Artillery Brigade
304th 305th 306th Field Artillery Regiments

304th 305th 306th Machine Gun Battalions

302nd Trench Mortar Battery
302nd Engineer Regiment
302nd Field Signal Battalion
302nd Division Train Headquarters & Military Police
302nd Supply Train
302nd Ammunition Train
302nd Engineer Train
302nd Sanitary Train
305th 306th 307th 308th Ambulance Companies & Field Hospitals

78th Division-National Army-1917

155th 156th Infantry Brigades
309th 310th 311th 312th Infantry Regiments

153rd Field Artillery Brigade
307th 308th 309th Field Artillery Regiments

307th 308th 309th Machine Gun Battalions

303rd Trench Mortar Battery
303rd Engineer Regiment
303rd Field Signal Battalion
303rd Division Train Headquarters & Military Police
303rd Supply Train
303rd Ammunition Train
303rd Engineer Train
303rd Sanitary Train
309th 310th 311th 312th Ambulance Companies & Field Hospitals

79th Division-National Army-Cross of Lorraine-1917

157th 158th Infantry Brigades
313th 314th 315th 316th Infantry Regiments

154th Field Artillery Brigade
310th 311th 312th Field Artillery Regiments

310th 311th 312th Machine Gun Battalions

304th Trench Mortar Battery
304th Engineer Regiment
304th Field Signal Battalion
304th Division Train Headquarters Military Police
304th Supply Train
304th Ammunition Train
304th Engineer Train
304th Sanitary Train
313th 314th 315th 316th Ambulance Companies & Field Hospitals

80th Division-National Army-Blue Ridge-1917

159th 160th Infantry Brigades
317th 318th 319th 320th Infantry Regiments

155th Field Artillery Brigade
313th 314th 315th Field Artillery Regiments

313th 314th 315th Machine Gun Battalions

305th Trench Mortar Battery
305th Engineer Regiment
305th Field Signal Battalion
305th Division Train Headquarters & Military Police
305th Supply Train
305th Ammunition Train
305th Engineer Train
305th Sanitary Train
317th 318th 319th 320th Ambulance Companies & Field Hospitals

81st Division-National Army-Wildcat-1917

161st 162nd Infantry Brigades
321st 322nd 323rd 324th Infantry Regiments

156th Field Artillery Brigade
316th 317th 318th Field Artillery Regiments

316th 317th 318th Machine Gun Battalions

306th Trench Mortar Battery
306th Engineer Regiment
306th Field Signal Battalion
306th Division Train Headquarters & Military Police
306th Supply Train
306th Ammunition Train
306th Engineer Train
306th Sanitary Train
321st 322nd 323rd 324th Ambulance Companies & Field Hopsitals

82nd Division-National Guard-All American-1917

163rd 164th Infantry Brigades
325th 326th 327th 328th Infantry Regiments

157th Field Artillery Brigade
319th 320th 321st Field Artillery Regiments

319th 320th 321st Machine Gun Battalions

307th Trench Mortar Battery
307th Engineer Regiment
307th Field Signal Battalion
307th Division Train Headquarters & Military Police
307th Supply Train
307th Ammunition Train
307th Engineer Train
307th Sanitary Train
325th 326th 327th 328th Ambulance Companies & Field Hospitals

83rd Division-National Army-Thunderbolt-1917

165th 166th Infantry Brigades
329th 330th 331st 332nd Infantry Regiments

158th Field Artillery Brigade
322nd 323rd 324th Field Artillery Regiments

322nd 323rd 324th Machine Gun Battalions

308th Trench Mortar Battery
308th Engineer Regiment
308th Field Signal Battalion
308th Division Train Headquarters & Military Police
308th Supply Train
308th Ammunition Train
308th Engineer Train
308th Sanitary Train
329th 330th 331st 332nd Ambulance Companies & Field Hospitals

84th Division-National Army-Railsplitters-1917

167th 168th Infantry Brigades
333rd 334th 335th 336th Infantry Regiments

159th Field Artillery Brigade
325th 326th 327th Field Artillery Regiments

325th 326th 327th Machine Gun Battalions

309th Trench Mortar Battery
309th Engineer Regiment
309th Division Train Headquarters & Military Police
309th Supply Train
309th Ammunition Train
309th Engineer Train
309th Sanitary Train
333rd 334th 335th 336th Ambulance Companies & Field Hospitals

85th Division-National Army-Custer-1917

169th 170th Infantry Brigades
337th 338th 339th 340th Infantry Regiments

160th Field Artillery Brigade
328th 329th 330th Field Artillery Regiments

328th 329th 330th Machine Gun Battalions

310th Trench Mortar Battery
310th Engineer Regiment
310th Field Signal Battalion
310th Division Train Headquarters & Military Police
310th Supply Train
310th Ammunition Train
310th Engineer Train
310th Sanitary Train
337th 338th 339th 340th Ambulance Companies & Field Hospitals

86th Division-National Army-Blackhawk-1917

171st 172nd Infantry Brigades
341st 342nd 343rd 344th Infantry Regiments

161st Field Artillery Brigade
331st 332nd 333rd Field Artillery Regiments

331st 332nd 333rd Machine Gun Battalions

311th Trench Mortar Battery
311th Engineer Regiment
311th Field Signal Battalion
311th Division Train Headquarters & Military Police
311th Supply Train
311th Ammunition Train
311th Engineer Train
311th Sanitary Train
341st 342nd 343rd 344th Ambulance Companies & Field Hospitals

87th Division-National Army-Acorn-1917

173rd 174th Infantry Brigades
345th 346th 347th 348th Infantry Regiments

162nd Field Artillery Brigade
334th 335th 336th Field Artillery Regiments

334th 335th 336th Machine Gun Battalions

312th Trench Mortar Battery
312th Engineer Regiment
312th Field Signal Battalion
312th Division Train Headquarters & Military Police
312th Supply Train
312th Ammunition Train
312th Engineer Train
312th Sanitary Train
345th 346th 347th 348th Ambulance Companies & Field Hospitals

88th Division-National Army-Blue Devils-1917

175th 176th Infantry Brigades
349th 350th 351st 352nd Infantry Regiments

163rd Field Artillery Brigade
337th 338th 339th Field Artillery Regiments

337th 338th 339th Machine Gun Battalions

313th Trench Mortar Battery
313th Engineer Regiment
313th Field Signal Battalion
313th Division Train Headquarters & Military Police
313th Supply Train
313th Ammunition Train
313th Engineer Train
313th Supply Train
349th 350th 351st 352nd Ambulance Companies & Field Hospitals

89th Division-National Army-Rolling W-1917

177th 178th Infantry Brigades
353rd 354th 355th 356th Infantry Regiments

164th Field Artillery Brigade
340th 341st 342nd Field Artillery Regiments

340th 341st 342nd Machine Gun Battalions

314th Trench Mortar Battery
314th Engineer Regiment
314th Field Signal Battalion
314th Division Train Headquarters & Military Police
314th Supply Train
314th Ammunition Train
314th Engineer Train
314th Sanitary Train
353rd 354th 355th 356th Ambulance Companies & Field Hospitals

90ᵗʰ Division-National Army-Tough Ombres-1917

179ᵗʰ 180ᵗʰ Infantry Brigades
357ᵗʰ 358ᵗʰ 359ᵗʰ 360ᵗʰ Infantry Regiments

165ᵗʰ Field Artillery Brigade
343ʳᵈ 344ᵗʰ 345ᵗʰ Field Artillery Regiments

343ʳᵈ 344ᵗʰ 345ᵗʰ Machine Gun Battalions

315ᵗʰ Trench Mortar Battery
315ᵗʰ Engineer Regiment
315ᵗʰ Field Signal Battalion
315ᵗʰ Supply Train
315ᵗʰ Ammunition Train
315ᵗʰ Engineer rain
315ᵗʰ Sanitary Train
357ᵗʰ 358ᵗʰ 359ᵗʰ 360ᵗʰ Ambulance Companies & Field Hospitals

91ˢᵗ Division-National Army-Powder River-1917

181ˢᵗ 182ⁿᵈ Infantry Brigades
361ˢᵗ 362ⁿᵈ 363ʳᵈ 364ᵗʰ Infantry Regiments

166ᵗʰ Field Artillery Brigade
346ᵗʰ 347ᵗʰ 348ᵗʰ Field Artillery Regiments

346ᵗʰ 347ᵗʰ 348ᵗʰ Machine Gun Battalions

316ᵗʰ Trench Mortar Battery
316ᵗʰ Engineer Regiment
316ᵗʰ Field Signal Battalion
316ᵗʰ Division Train Headquarters Military Police
316ᵗʰ Supply Train
316ᵗʰ Ammunition Train
316ᵗʰ Engineer Train
316ᵗʰ Sanitary Train
361ˢᵗ 362ⁿᵈ 363ʳᵈ 364ᵗʰ Ambulance Companies & Field Hospital

93rd Division-National Army-Bloody Hand-1917

185th 186th Infantry Brigades
369th 370th 371st 372nd Infantry Regiments

The rest of the division was not organized.

95th Division-National Army-Victory-1918

189th 190th Infantry Brigades
377th 378th 379th 380th Infantry Regiments

170th Field Artillery Brigade
358th 359th 360th Field Artillery Regiments

358th 359th 360th Machine Gun Battalions

320th Trench Mortar Battery
320th Engineer Regiment
620th Field Signal Battalion
320th Division Train Headquarters & Military Police
320th Supply Train
320th Ammunition Train
320th Engineer Train
320th Sanitary Train
377th 378th 379th 380th Ambulance Companies & Field Hospital

93rd Division-National Army-Bloody Hand-1917

185th 186th Infantry Brigades
369th 370th 371st 372nd Infantry Regiments

The rest of the division was not organized.

95th Division-National Army-Victory-1918

189th 190th Infantry Brigades
377th 378th 379th 380th Infantry Regiments

170th Field Artillery Brigade
358th 359th 360th Field Artillery Regiments

358th 359th 360th Machine Gun Battalions

320th Trench Mortar Battery
320th Engineer Regiment
620th Field Signal Battalion
320th Division Train Headquarters & Military Police
320th Supply Train
320th Ammunition Train
320th Engineer Train
320th Sanitary Train
377th 378th 379th 380th Ambulance Companies & Field Hospital

96th Division-National Army-Deadeyes-1918

191st 192nd Infantry Brigades
381st 382nd 383rd 384th Infantry Regiments

171st Field Artillery Brigade
361st 362nd 363rd Field Artillery Regiments

361st 362nd 363rd Machine Gun Battalions

321st Trench Mortar Battery
321st Engineer Regiment
621st Field Signal Battalion
321st Division Train Headquarters & Military Police
321st Supply Train
321st Ammunition Train
321st Engineer Train
321st Sanitary Train
381st 382nd 383rd 384th Ambulance Companies & Field Hopsitals

97th Division-National Army-Trident-1918

193rd 194th Infantry Brigades
385th 386th 387th 388th Infantry Regiments

172nd Field Artillery Brigade
364th 365th 366th Field Artillery Regiments

364th 365th 366th Machine Gun Battalions

322nd Trench Mortar Battery
322nd Engineer Regiment
622nd Field Signal Battalion
322nd Division Train Headquarters & Military Police
322nd Supply Train
322nd Ammunition Train
322nd Engineer Train
322nd Sanitary Train
385th 386th 387th 388th Ambulance Companies & Field Hospitals

98th Division-National Army-Iroquois-1918

195th 196th Infantry Brigades
389th 390th 391st 392nd Infantry Regiments

173rd Field Artillery Brigade
367th 368th 369th Field Artillery Regiments

367th 368th 369th Machine Gun Battalions

323rd Trench Mortar Battery
323rd Engineer Regiment
623rd Field Signal Battalion
323rd Division Train Headquarters & Military Police
323rd Supply Train
323rd Ammunition Train
323rd Engineer Train
323rd Supply Train
389th 390th 391st 392nd Ambulance Companies & Field Hospitals

99th Division-National Army-Checkerboard-1918

197th 198th Infantry Brigades
393rd 394th 395th 396th Infantry Regiments

174th Field Artillery Brigade
370th 371st 372nd Field Artillery Regiments

370th 371st 372nd Machine Gun Battalions

324th Trench Mortar Battery
324th Engineer Regiment
624th Field Signal Battalion
324th Division Train Headquarters & Military Police
324th Supply Train
324th Ammunition Train
324th Engineer Train
324th Sanitary Train
393rd 394th 395th 396th Ambulance Companies & Field Hospitals

100th Division-National Army-Century-1918

199th 200th Infantry Brigades
397th 398th 399th 400th Infantry Regiments

175th Field Artillery Brigade
373rd 374th 375th Field Artillery Regiments

373rd 374th 375th Machine Gun Battalions

325th Trench Mortar Battery
325th Engineer Regiment
625th Field Signal Battalion
325th Division Train Headquarters & Military Police
325th Supply Train
325th Ammunition Train
325th Engineer Train
325th Sanitary Train
397th 398th 399th 400th Ambulance Companies & Field Hospitals

101st Division-national Army-Screaming Eagles-1918

201st 202nd Infantry Brigades
401st 402nd 403rd 404th Infantry Regiments

176th Field Artillery Brigade
376th 377th 378th Field Artillery Regiments

376th 377th 378th Machine Gun Battalions

326th Trench Mortar Battery
326th Engineer Regiment
626th Field Signal Battalion
326th Division Train Headquarters & Military Police
326th Supply Train
326th Ammunition Train
326th Engineer Train
326th Sanitary Train
401st 402nd 403rd 404th Ambulance Companies & Field Hospitals

102nd Division-National Army-Ozark-1918

203rd 204th Infantry Brigades
405th 406th 407th 408th Infantry Regiments

177th Field Artillery Brigade
379th 380th 381st Field Artillery Regiments

379th 380th 381st Machine Gun Battalions

327th Trench Mortar Battery
327th Engineer Regiment
627th Field Signal Battalion
327th Division Train Headquarters & Military Police
327th Supply Train
327th Ammunition Train
327th Engineer Train
327th Sanitary Train
405th 406th 407th 408th Ambulance Companies & Field Hospitals

Provisional Division-National Army-Puerto Rico-1918

187th 188th Infantry Brigades
373rd 374th 375th 376th Infantry Regiments

The rest of the division was not organized.

1945

1st Infantry Division-Active Component-Big Red One-1945

16th 18th 26th Infantry Regiments

5th 7th 32nd 33rd Field Artillery Battalions

1st Signal Company
701st Ordnance Company
1st Quartermaster Company
1st Reconnaissance Troop
1st Engineer Battalion
1st Medical Battalion
1st Military Police Platoon
1st CIC Detachment

2nd Infantry Division-Active Component-Indianhead-1945

9th 23rd 38th Infantry Regiments

12th 15th 37th 38th Field Artillery Battalions

2nd Signal Company
702nd Ordnance Company
2nd Quartermaster Company
2nd Reconnaissance Troop
2nd Engineer Battalion
2nd Medical Battalion
2nd Military Police Platoon
2nd CIC Detachment

3rd Infantry Division-Active Component-Marne-1945

7th 15th 30th Infantry Regiments

9th 10th 39th 41st Field Artillery Battalions

3rd Signal Company
703rd Ordnance Company
3rd Quartermaster Company
3rd Reconnaissance Troop
10th Engineer Battalion
3rd Medical Battalion
3rd Military Police Platoon
3rd CIC Detachment

4th Infantry Division-Active Component-Ivy-1945

8th 12th 22nd Infantry Regiments

20th 29th 42nd 44th Field Artillery Battalions

4th Signal Company
704th Ordnance Company
4th Quartermaster Company
4th Reconnaissance Troop
4th Engineer Battalion
4th Medical Battalion
4th Military Police Platoon
4th CIC Detachment

5th Infantry Division-Active Component-Red Devils-1945

2nd 10th 11th Infantry Regiments

19th 21st 46th 50th Field Artillery Battalions

5th Signal Company
705th Ordnance Company
5th Quartermaster Company
5th Reconnaissance Troop
7th Engineer Battalion
5th Medical Battalion
5th Military Police Platoon
5th CIC Detachment

6th Airborne Division-Phantom Division-Army of the U.S.-1945

Subdivisional Components remained a complete fiction.

7th Infantry Division-Active Component-Bayonet-1945

17th 31st 184th Infantry Regiments

31st 48th 49th 57th Field Artillery Battalions

7th Signal Company
707th Ordnance Company
7th Quartermaster Company
7th Reconnaissance Troop
13th Engineer Battalion
7th Medical Battalion
7th Military Police Platoon
7th CIC Detachment

8th Infantry Division-Active Component-Pathfinders-1945

13th 28th 121st Infantry Regiments

28th 43rd 45th 56th Field Artillery Battalions

8th Signal Company
708th Ordnance Company
8th Quartermaster Company
8th Reconnaissance Troop
12th Engineer Battalion
8th Medical Battalion
8th Military Police Platoon
8th CIC Detachment

9th Airborne Division-Phantom Division-Army of the U.S.-1945

Subdivisional Components remained a complete fiction.

9th Infantry Division-Active Component-Varsity-1945

39th 47th 60th Infantry Regiments

26th 34th 60th 84th Field Artillery Battalions

9th Signal Company
709th Ordnance Company
9th Quartermaster Company
9th Reconnaissance Troop
15th Engineer Battalion
9th Medical Battalion
9th Military Police Platoon
9th CIC Detachment

10th Mountain Division-Active Component-Mountaineers-1945

85th 86th 87th Infantry Regiments

604th 605th 616th Field Artillery Battalions

110th Signal Company
710th Ordnance Company
10th Quartermaster Company
10th Reconnaissance Troop
126th Engineer Battalion
10th Medical Battalion
10th Military police Platoon
10th CIC Detachment

11th Airborne Division-Active Component-Angels-1945

187th Glider Infantry Regiment
188th 511th Parachute Infantry Regiments

472nd 675th Glider Field Artillery Battalions
457th 674th Parachute Field Artillery Battalions

152nd Antiaircraft Artillery Battalion

11th Parachute Maintenance Company
511th Signal Company
711th Ordnance Company
408th Quartermaster Company
127th Engineer Battalion
221st Medical Company
11th Military Police Platoon

11th Infantry Division-Phantom Division-Army of the U.S.-1945

Subdivisional Components remained a complete fiction.

12th Infantry Division-Active Component-Phillipine-1946

43rd 45th 57th Infantry Regiments

23rd 24th 85th 86th Field Artillery Battalions

12th Signal Company
12th Ordnance Company
12th Quartermaster Company
12th Reconnaissance Troop
41st Engineer Battalion
12th Medical Battalion
12th Military Police Platoon
12th CIC Detachment

13th Airborne Division-Army of the U.S.-1945

326th Glider Infantry Regiment
515th 517th Parachute Infantry Regiments

676th 677th Glider Field Artillery Battalions
458th 460th Parachute Field Artillery Battalions

153rd Antiaircraft Artillery Battalion

13th Parachute Maintenance Company
513th Signal Company

713th Ordnance Company
409th Quartermaster Company
129th Engineer Battalion
224th Medical Company
13th Military Police Platoon

14th Infantry Division-Phantom Division-Army of the U.S.-1945

Subdivisional Components remained a complete fiction.

15th Airborne Division-Constituted-Army of the U.S.-1945

191st 192nd Glider Infantry Regiments
545th Parachute Infantry Regiment

678th 679th Glider Field Artillery Battalions
459th Parachute Field Artillery Battalion

154th Antiaircraft Artillery Battalion

15th Parachute Maintenance Company
515th Signal Company
715th Ordnance Company
410th Quartermaster Company
131st Engineer Battalion
223rd Medical Company
15th Military Police Platoon

17th Airborne Division-Army of the U.S.-Golden Talon-1945

194th Glider Infantry Regiment
507th 513th Parachute Infantry Regiments

680th 681st Glider Field Artillery Battalions
464th 466th Parachute Field Artillery Battalions

155th Antiaircraft Artillery Battalion

17th Parachute Maintenance Company
517th signal Company
717th Ordnance Company

411th Quartermaster Company
139th Engineer Battalion
224th Medical Company
17th Military Police Platoon

18th Airborne Division-Phantom Division-Army of the U.S.-1945

Subdivisional Components remained a complete fiction.

21st Airborne Division-Phantom Division-Army of the U.S.-1945

Subdivisional Components remained a complete fiction.

22nd Infantry Division-Phantom Division-Army of the U.S.-1945

Subdivisional Components remained a complete fiction.

Americal Division-Army of the U.S.-Americal-1945

132nd 164th 182nd Infantry Regiments

221st 245th 246th 247th Field Artillery Battalions

26th Signal Company
721st Ordnance Company
125th Quartermaster Company
21st Reconnaissance Troop
57th Engineer Battalion
121st Medical Company
Military Police Platoon
182nd CIC Detachment

24th Infantry Division-Active Component-Victory-1945

19th 21st 34th Infantry Regiments

11th 13th 52nd 63rd Field Artillery Battalions

24th Signal Company
724th Ordnance Company
24th Quartermaster Company
24th Reconnaissance Troop
3rd Medical Battalion
24th Medical Battalion
24th Military Police Platoon
24th CIC Detachment

25th Infantry Division-Active Component-Tropic Lightning-1945

27th 35th 161st Infantry Regiments

8th 64th 89th 90th Field Artillery Battalions

25th Signal Company
725th Ordnance Company
25th Quartermaster Company
25th Reconnaissance Troop
65th Engineer Battalion
25th Medical Battalion
25th Military Police Platoon
25th CIC Detachment

26th Infantry Division-National Guard-Yankee-1945

101st 104th 328th Infantry Regiments

101st 102nd 180th 263rd Field Artillery Battalions

39th Signal Company
726th Ordnance Company
26th Quartermaster Company
26th Reconnaissance Troop

101st Engineer Battalion
114th Medical Battalion
26th Military Police Platoon
26th CIC Detachment

27th Infantry Division-National Guard-New York-1945

105th 106th 165th Infantry Regiments

104th 105th 106th 249th Field Artillery Battalions

27th Signal Company
727th Ordnance Company
27th Quartermaster Company
27th Reconnaissance Troop
102nd Engineer Battalion
102nd Medical Battalion
27th Military Police Platoon
27th CIC Detachment

28th Infantry Division-National Guard-Keystone-1945

109th 110th 112th Infantry Regiments

107th 108th 109th 229th Field Artillery Battalions

28th Signal Company
728th Ordnance Company
28th Quartermaster Company
28th Reconnaissance Troop
103rd Engineer Battalion
103rd Medical Battalion
28th Military Police Platoon
28th CIC Detachment

29th Infantry Division-National Guard-Blue & Gray-1945

115th 116th 175th Infantry Regiments

110th 111th 224th 227th Field Artillery Battalions

29th Signal Company
729th Ordnance Company
29th Quartermaster Company
29th Reconnaissance Troop
121st Engineer Battalion
104th Medical Battalion
29th Military Police Platoon
29th CIC Detachment

30th Infantry Division-National Guard-Old Hickory-1945

117th 119th 120th Infantry Regiments

113th 115th 197th 230th Field Artillery Battalions

30th Signal Company
730th Ordnance Company
30th Quartermaster Company
30th Reconnaissance Troop
105th Engineer Battalion
105th Medical Battalion
30th Military Police Platoon
30th CIC Detachment

31st Infantry Division-National Guard-Dixie-1945

124th 155th 167th Infantry Regiments

114th 116th 117th 149th Field Artillery Battalions

31st Signal Company
731st Ordnance Company
31st Quartermaster Company
31st Reconnaissance Troop

106th Engineer Battalion
106th Medical Battalion
31st Military Police Platoon
31st CIC Detachment

32nd Infantry Division-National Guard-Red Arrow-1945

126th 127th 128th Infantry Regiments

120th 121st 126th 129th Field Artillery Battalions

32nd Signal Company
732nd Ordnance Company
32nd Quartermaster Company
32nd Reconnaissance Troop
114th Engineer Battalion
107th Medical Battalion
32nd Military Police Platoon
32nd CIC Detachment

33rd Infantry Division-National Guard-Prairie-1945

123rd 130th 136th Infantry Regiments

122nd 123rd 124th 210th Field Artillery Battalions

33rd Signal Company
733rd Ordnance Company
33rd Quartermaster Company
33rd Reconnaissance Troop
108th Engineer Battalion
108th Medical Battalion
33rd Military Police Platoon
33rd CIC Detachment

34th Infantry Division-National Guard-Red Bull-1945

133rd 135th 168th Infantry Regiments

125th 151st 175th 185th Field Artillery Battalions

34th Signal Company
734th Ordnance Company
34th Quartermaster Company
34th Reconnaissance Troop
109th Engineer Battalion
109th Medical Battalion
34th Military Police Platoon
34th CIC Detachment

35th Infantry Division-National Guard-Santa Fe-1945

134th 137th 320th Infantry Regiments

127th 161st 216th 219th Field Artillery Battalions

35th Signal Company
735th Ordnance Company
35th Quartermaster Company
35th Reconnaissance Troop
60th Engineer Battalion
110th Medical Battalion
35th Military Police Platoon
35th CIC Detachment

36th Infantry Division-National Guard-Texas-1945

141st 142nd 143rd Infantry Regiments

131st 132nd 133rd 155th Field Artillery Battalions

36th Signal Company
736th Ordnance Company
36th Quartermaster Company
36th Reconnaissance Troop
111th Engineer Battalion
111th Medical Battalion
36th Military Police Platoon
36th CIC Detachment

37th Infantry Division-National Guard-Buckeye-1945

129th 145th 148th Infantry Regiments

6th 135th 136th 140th Field Artillery Battalions

37th Signal Company
737th Ordnance Company
37th Quartermaster Company
37th Reconnaissance Troop
112th Engineer Battalion
112th Medical Battalion
37th Military Police Platoon
37th CIC Detachment

38th Infantry Division-National Guard-Cyclone-1945

149th 151st 152nd Infantry Regiments

138th 139th 150th 163rd Field Artillery Battalions

38th Signal Company
738th Ordnance Company
38th Quartermaster Company
38th Reconnaissance Troop
113th Engineer Battalion
113th Medical Battalion
38th Military Police Platoon
38th CIC Detachment

39th Infantry Division-National Guard-Delta-1945

Division was not organized during WW2

40th Infantry Division-National Guard-Sunrise-1945

108th 160th 185th Infantry Regiments

143rd 164th 213th 222nd Field Artillery Battalions

40th Signal Company
740th Ordnance Company
40th Quartermaster Company
40th Reconnaissance Troop
115th Engineer Battalion
115th Medical Battalion
40th Military Police Platoon
40th CIC Detachment

41st Infantry Division-National Guard-Sunset-1945

162nd 163rd 186th Infantry Regiments

146th 147th 205th 218th Field Artillery Battalions

41st Signal Company
741st Ordnance Company
41st Quartermaster Company
41st Reconnaissance Troop
116th Engineer Battalion
116th Medical Battalion
41st Military Police Platoon
41st CIC Detachment

42nd Infantry Division-Army of the U.S.-Rainbow-1945

222nd 232nd 242nd Infantry Regiments

232nd 292nd 402nd 542nd Field Artillery Battalions

42nd Signal Company
742nd Ordnance Company
42nd Quartermaster Company
42nd Reconnaissance Troop
142nd Engineer Battalion
122nd Medical Battalion
42nd Military Police Platoon
42nd CIC Detachment

43rd Infantry Division-National Guard-Red Wing-1945

103rd 169th 172nd Infantry Regiments

103rd 152nd 169th 172nd Field Artillery Battalions

43rd Signal Company
743rd Ordnance Company
43rd Quartermaster Company
43rd Reconnaissance Troop
118th Engineer Battalion
118th Medical Battalion
43rd Military Police Platoon
43rd CIC Detachment

44th Infantry Division-National Guard-1945

71st 114th 324th Infantry Regiments

156th 157th 217th 220th Field Artillery Battalions

44th Signal Company
744th Ordnance Company
44th Quartermaster Company
44th Reconnaissance Troop63rd Engineer Battalion
119th Medical Battalion
44th Military Police Platoon
44th CIC Detachment

45th Infantry Division-National Guard-Thunderbird-1945

157th 179th 180th Infantry Regiments

158th 160th 171st 189th Field Artillery Battalions

45th Signal Company
745th Ordnance Company
45th Quartermaster Company
45th Reconnaissance Troop
120th Engineer Battalion

120th Medical Battalion
45th Military Police Platoon
45th CIC Detachment

46th Infantry Division-Phantom Division-Army of the U.S.-1945

Subdivisional components remained a complete fiction.S

48th Infantry Division-Phantom Division-Army of the U.S.-1945

Subdivisional components remained a complete fiction.

48th Infantry Division-Phantom Division-Army of the U.S.-1945

Subdivisional components remained a complete fiction.
50th Infantry Division-Phantom Division-Army of the U.S.-1945

Subdivisional components remained a complete fiction.
55th Infantry Division-Phantom Division-Army of the U.S.-1945

Subdivisional components remained complete fiction

59th Infantry Division-Phantom Division-Army of the U.S.-1945

Subdivisional components remained a complete fiction.

61st Infantry Division-Constituted-Army of the U.S.-1945

247th 248th 249th Infantry Regiments

716th 855th 856th 857th Field Artillery Battalions

561st Signal Company
761st Ordnance Company
61st Quartermaster Company
61st Reconnaissance Troop

261st Engineer Battalion
361st Medical Battalion
61st Military Police Platoon
61st CIC Detachment

62nd Infantry Division-Constituted-Army of the United States-1945

250th 251st 252nd Infantry Regiments

717th 858th 859th 860th Field Artillery Battalions

562nd Signal Company
762nd Ordnance Company
62nd Quartermaster Company
62nd Reconnaissance Troop
262nd Engineer Battalion
362nd Medical Battalion
62nd Military Police Platoon
62nd CIC Detachment

63rd Infantry Division-Army of the U.S.-Blood & Fire-1945

253rd 254th 255th Infantry Regiments

718th 861st 862nd 863rd Field Artillery Battalions

563rd Signal Company
763rd Ordnance Company
63rd Quartermaster Company
63rd Reconnaissance Troop
263rd Engineer Battalion
363rd Medical Battalion
63rd Military Police Platoon
63rd CIC Detachment

65th Infantry Division-Army of the U.S.-Battle Axe-1945

259th 260th 261st Infantry Regiments

720th 867th 868th 869th Field Artillery Battalions

565th Signal Company
765th Ordnance Company
65th Quartermaster Company
65th Reconnaissance Troop
265th Engineer Battalion
365th Medical Battalion
65th Military Police Platoon
65th CIC Detachment

66th Infantry Division-Army of the U.S.-Panther-1945

262nd 263rd 264th Infantry Regiments

721st 870th 871st 872nd Field Artillery Battalions

566th Signal Company
766th Ordnance Company
66th Quartermaster Company
66th Reconnaissance Troop
266th Engineer Battalion
366th Medical Battalion
66th Military Police Platoon
66th CIC Detachment

67th Infantry Division-Constituted-Army of the U.S.-1945

265th 266th 267th Infantry Regiments

722nd 873rd 874th 875th Field Artillery Battalions

567th Signal Company
767th Ordnance Company
67th Quartermaster Company
67th Reconnaissance Troop
67th Military Police Platoon
67th CIC Detachmen

68th Infantry Division-Constituted-Army of the U.S.-1945

268th 269th 270th Infantry Regiments

723rd 876th 877th 878th Field Artillery Battalions

568th Signal Company
768th Ordnance Company
68th Quartermaster Company
68th Reconnaissance Troop
268th Engineer Battalion
368th Medical Battalion
68th Military Police Platoon
68th CIC Detachment

69th Infantry Division-Army of the U.S.-Fighting 69th-1945

271st 272nd 273rd Infantry Regiments

724th 879th 880th 881st Field Artillery Battalions

569th Signal Company
769th Ordnance Company
69th Quartermaster Company
69th Reconnaissance Troop
269th Engineer Battalion
369th Medical Battalion
69th Military Police Platoon
69th CIC Detachment

70th Infantry Division-Army of the U.S.-Trailblazer-1945

274th 275th 276th Infantry Regiments

725th 882nd 883rd 884th Field Artillery Battalions

570th Signal Company
770th Ordnance Company
70th Quartermaster Company
70th Reconnaissance Troop

270th Engineer Battalion
370th Medical Battalion
70th Military Police Platoon
70th CIC Detachment

71st Infantry Division-Army of the U.S.-Red Circle-1945

5th 14th 66th Infantry Regiments

564th 607th 608th 609th Field Artillery Battalions

571st Signal Company
771st Ordnance Company
251st Quartermaster Company
71st Reconnaissance Troop
271st Engineer Battalion
371st Medical Battalion
71st Military Police Platoon
71st CIC Detachment

72nd Infantry Division-Constituted-Army of the U.S.-1945

280th 281st 282nd Infantry Regiments

727th 888th 889th 890th Field Artillery Battalions

572nd Signal Company
772nd Ordnance Company
72nd Quartermaster Company
72nd Reconnaissance Troop
272nd Engineer Battalion
372nd Medical Battalion
72nd Military Police Platoon
72nd CIC Detachment

73rd Infantry Division-Constituted-Army of the U.S.-1945

283rd 284th 285th Infantry Regiments

728th 891st 892nd 893rd Field Artillery Battalions

573rd Signal Company
773rd Ordnance Company
73rd Quartermaster Company
73rd Reconnaissance Troop
273rd Engineer Battalion
373rd Medical Battalion
73rd Military Police Platoon
73rd CIC Detachment

74th Infantry Division-Constituted-Army of the U.S.-1945

286th 287th 288th Infantry Regiments

729th 894th 895th 896th Field Artillery Battalions
574th Signal Company
774th Ordnance Company
74th Quartermaster Company
74th Reconnaissance Troop
274th Engineer Battalion
374th Medical Battalion
74th Military Police Platoon
74th CIC Detachment

75th Infantry Division-Army of the U.S.-1945

289th 290th 291st Infantry Regiments

730th 897th 898th 899th Field Artillery Battalions

575th Signal Company
775th Ordnance Company
75th Quartermaster Company
75th Reconnaissance Troop

275th Engineer Battalion
375th Medical Battalion
75th Military Police Platoon
75th CIC Detachment

76th Infantry Division-Army Reserve-Onaway-1945

304th 385th 417th Infantry Regiments

302nd 355th 364th 901st Field Artillery Battalions

76th Signal Company
776th Ordnance Company
76th Quartermaster Company
76th Reconnaissance Troop
301st Engineer Battalion
301st Medical Battalion
76th Military Police Platoon
76th CIC Detachment

77th Infantry Division-Army Reserve-Statue of Liberty-1945

305th 306th 307th Infantry Regiments

304th 305th 306th 902nd Field Artillery Battalions

77th Signal Company
77th Ordnance Company
77th Quartermaster Company
77th Reconnaissance Troop
302nd Engineer Battalion
302nd Medical Battalion
77th Military Police Platoon
77th CIC Detachment

78th Infantry Division-Army Reserve-Lightning-1945

309th 310th 311th Infantry Regiments

307th 308th 309th 903rd Field Artillery Battalions

78th Signal Company
778th Ordnance Company
78th Quartermaster Company
78th Reconnaissance Troop
303rd Engineer Battalion
303rd Medical Battalion
78th Military Police Platoon
78th CIC Detachment

79th Infantry Division-Army Reserve-Cross of Lorraine-1945

313th 314th 315th Infantry Regiments

310th 311th 312th 904th Field Artillery Battalions

79th Signal Company
779th Ordnance Company
79th Quartermaster Company
79th Reconnaissance Troop
304th Engineer Battalion304th Medical Battalion
79th Military Police Platoon
79th CIC Detachment

80th Infantry Division-Army Reserve-Blue Ridge-1945

317th 318th 319th Infantry Regiments

313th 314th 315th 905th Field Artillery Battalions

80th Signal Company
780th Ordnance Company
80th Quartermaster Company
80th Reconnaissance Troop
305th Engineer Battalion
305th Medical Battalion
80th Military Police Platoon
80th CIC Detachment

81st Infantry Division-Army Reserve-Wildcat-1945

321st 322nd 323rd Infantry Regiments

316th 317th 318th 906th Field Artillery Battalions

81st Signal Company
781st Ordnance Company
81st Quartermaster Company
81st Reconnaissance Troop
306th Engineer Battalion
306th Medical Battalion
81st Military Police Platoon
81st CIC Detachment

82nd Airborne Division-Active Component-All American-1945

325th Glider Infantry Regiment
504th 505th Parachute Infantry Regiment

319th 320th Glider Field Artillery Battalions
376th 456th Parachute Field Artillery Battalions

80th Antiaircraft Artillery Battalion

82nd Parachute Maintenance Company
82nd Signal Company
782nd Ordnance Company
407th Quartermaster Company
307th Engineer Battalion
307th Medical Battalion
82nd military Police Platoon

83rd Infantry Division-Army Reserve-Thunderbolt-1945

329th 330th 331st Infantry Regiments

322nd 323rd 324th 908th Field Artillery Battalions

83rd Signal Company

783rd Ordnance Company
83rd Quartermaster Company
83rd Reconnaissance Troop
308th Engineer Battalion
308th Medical Battalion
83rd CIC Detachment

84th Infantry Division-Army Reserve-Railsplitters-1945

333rd 334th 335th Infantry Regiments

325th 326th 327th 909th Field Artillery Battalions

84th Signal Company
784th Ordnance Company
84th Quartermaster Company
84th Reconnaissance Troop
309th Engineer Battalion
309th Medical Battalion
84th Military Police Platoon
84th CIC Detachment

85th Infantry Division-Army Reserve-Custer-1945

337th 338th 339th Infantry Regiments

328th 329th 403rd 910th Field Artillery Battalions

85th Signal Company
785th Ordnance Company
85th Quartermaster Company
85th Reconnaissance Troop
310th Engineer Battalion
310th Medical Battalion
85th Military Police Platoon
85th CIC Detachment

86th Infantry Division-Army Reserve-Blackhawk-1945

341st 342nd 343rd Infantry Regiments

331st 332nd 404th 911th Field Artillery Battalions

86th Signal Company
786th Ordnance Company
86th Quartermaster Company
86th Reconnaissance Troop
311th Engineer Battalion
311th Medical Battalion
86th Military Police Platoon
86th CIC Detachment

87th Infantry Division-Army Reserve-Acorn-1945

345th 346th 347th Infantry Regiments

334th 335th 336th 912th Field Artillery Battalions

87th Signal Company
787th Ordnance Company
87th Quartermaster Company
87th Reconnaissance Troop
312th Engineer Battalion312th Medical Battalion
87th Military Police Platoon
87th CIC Detachment

88th Infantry Division-Army Reserve-Blue Devils-1945

349th 350th 351st Infantry Regiments

337th 338th 339th 913th Field Artillery Battalions

88th Signal Company
788th Ordnance Company
88th Quartermaster Company
88th Reconnaissance Troop
313th Engineer Battalion

313th Medical Battalion
88th Military Police Platoon
88th CIC Detachment

89th Infantry Division-Army Reserve-Rolling W-1945

353rd 354th 355th Infantry Regiments

340th 341st 563rd 914th Field Artillery Battalions

89th Signal Company
789th Ordnance Company
89th Quartermaster Company
89th Reconnaissance Troop
314th Engineer Battalion
314th Medical Battalion
89th Military Police Platoon
89th CIC Detachment

90th Infantry Division-Army Reserve-Tough Ombres-1945

357th 358th 359th Infantry Regiments

343rd 344th 345th 915th Field Artillery Battalions
90th Signal Company
790th Ordnance Company
90th Quartermaster Company
90th Reconnaissance Troop
315th Engineer Battalion
315th Medical Battalion
90th Military Police Platoon
90th CIC Detachment

91st Infantry Division-Army Reserve-Powder River-1945

345th 346th 347th Infantry Regiments

346th 347th 348th 916th Field Artillery Battalions

91st Signal Company
791st Ordnance Company
91st Quartermaster Company
91st Reconnaissance Troop
316th Engineer Battalion
316th Medical Battalion
91st Military Police Platoon
91st CIC Detachment

92nd Infantry Division-Army of the U.S.-Buffalo-1945

365th 370th 371st Infantry Regiments

597th 598th 599th 600th Field Artillery Battalions

92nd Signal Company
792nd Ordnance Company
92nd Quartermaster Company
92nd Reconnaissance Troop
317th Engineer Battalion
317th Medical Battalion
92nd Military Police Platoon
92nd CIC Detachment

93rd Infantry Division-Army of the U.S.-Bloody Hand-1945

25th 368th 369th Infantry Regiments

593rd 594th 595th 596th Field Artillery Battalions

93rd Signal Company
793rd Ordnance Company
93rd Quartermaster Company
93rd Reconnaissance Troop
318th Engineer Battalion
318th Medical Battalion
93rd Military Police Platoon
93rd CIC Detachment

94th Infantry Division-Army Reserve-Nuef Quatres-1945

301st 302nd 376th Infantry Regiments

301st 356th 390th 919th Field Artillery Battalions

94th Signal Company
794th Ordnance Company
94th Quartermaster Company
94th Reconnaissance Troop
319th Engineer Battalion
319th Medical Battalion
94th Military Police Platoon
94th CIC Detachment

95th Infantry Division-Army Reserve-Iron Men of Metz-1945

377th 378th 379th Infantry Regiments

358th 359th 360th 920th Field Artillery Battalions

95th Signal Company
795th Ordnance Company
95th Quartermaster Company
95th Reconnaissance Troop
320th Engineer Battalion320[th] Medical Battalion
95th Military Police Platoon
95th CIC Detachment

96th Infantry Division-Army Reserve-Deadeyes-1945

381st 382nd 383rd Infantry Regiments

361st 362nd 363rd 921st Field Artillery Battalions

96th Signal Company
796th Ordnance Company
96th Quartermaster Company
96th Reconnaissance Troop

321st Engineer Battalion
321st Medical Battalion
96th Military Police Platoon
96th CIC Detachment

97th Infantry Division-Army Reserve-Trident-1945

303rd 386th 387th Infantry Regiments

303rd 365th 389th 922nd Field Artillery Battalions

97th Signal Company
797th Ordnance Company
97th Quartermaster Company
97th Reconnaissance Troop
322nd Engineer Battalion
322nd Medical Battalion
97th Military Police Platoon
97th CIC Detachment

98th Infantry Division-Army Reserve-Iroquois-1945

389th 390th 391st Infantry Regiments

367th 368th 399th 923rd Field Artillery Battalions98th Signal Company
798th Ordnance Company
98th Quartermaster Company
98th Reconnaissance Troop
323rd Engineer Battalion
323rd Medical Battalion
98th Military Police Platoon
98th CIC Detachment

99th Infantry Division-Army Reserve-Checkerboard-1945

393rd 394th 395th Infantry Regiments

370th 371st 372nd 924th Field Artillery Battalions

99th Signal Company
799th Ordnance Company
99th Quartermaster Company
99th Reconnaissance Troop
324th Engineer Battalion
324th Medical Battalion
99th Military Police Platoon
99th CIC Detachment

100th Infantry Division-Army Reserve-Century-1945

397th 398th 399th Infantry Regiments

373rd 374th 375th 925th Field Artillery Battalions

100th Signal company
800th Ordnance Company
100th Quartermaster Company
100th Reconnaissance Troop
325th Engineer Battalion
325th Medical Battalion
100th Military Police Platoon
100th CIC Detachment

101st Airborne Division-Active Component-Screaming Eagles-1945

327th Glider Infantry Regiment
502nd 506th Parachute Infantry Regiments

321st 907th Glider Field Artillery Battalions
377th 463rd Parachute Field Artillery Battalions

81st Antiaircraft Artillery Battalion

101st Parachute Maintenance Company
101st Signal Company
801st Ordnance Company
426th Quartermaster Company
326th Engineer Battalion
326th Medical Company
101st Military Police Platoon

102nd Infantry Division-Army Reserve-Ozark-1945

405th 406th 407th Infantry Regiments

379th 380th 381st 927th Field Artillery Battalions

102nd Signal Company
802nd Ordnance Company
102nd Quartermaster Company
102nd Reconnaissance Troop
327th Engineer Battalion
327th Medical Battalion
102nd Military Police Platoon
102nd CIC Detachment

103rd Infantry Division-Army Reserve-Catcus-1945

409th 410th 411th Infantry Regiments

382nd 383rd 384th 928th Field Artillery Battalions

103rd Signal Company
803rd Ordnance Company 103rd Quartermaster Company
103rd Reconnaissance Troop
328th Engineer Battalion
328th Medical Battalion
103rd Military Police Platoon
103rd CIC Detachment

104th Infantry Division-Army Reserve-Timberwolves-1945

413th 414th 415th Infantry Regiments

385th 386th 387th 929th Field Artillery Battalions

104th Signal Company
804th Ordnance Company
104th Quartermaster Company
104th Reconnaissance Troop
329th Engineer Battalion
104th Medical Battalion
104th Military Police Platoon
104th CIC Detachment

105th Infantry Division-Constituted-Army of the U.S.-1945

419th 420th 421st Infantry Regiments

585th 586th 587th 588th Field Artillery Battalions

105th Signal Company
805th Ordnance Company
105th Quartermaster Company
105th Reconnaissance Troop
330th Engineer Battalion
330th Medical Battalion
105th Military Police Platoon
105th CIC Detachment

106th Infantry Division-Army of the U.S.-Golden Lion-1945

422nd 423rd 424th Infantry Regiments

589th 590th 592nd 593rd Field Artillery Battalions

106th Signal Company
806th Ordnance Company
106th Quartermaster Company

108th Reconnaissance Troop
81st Engineer Battalion
331st Medical Battalion
106th Military Police Platoon
106th CIC Detachment

107th Infantry Division-Constituted-Army of the U.S.-1945

308th 312th 316th Infantry Regiments

The rest of the division was not constituted.

108th Infantry Division-Phantom Division-Army of the U.S.-1945

Subdivisional components remained a complete fiction.

119th Infantry Division-Phantom Division-Army of the U.S.-1945

Subdivisional components remained a complete fiction.

130th Infantry Division-Phantom Division-Army of the U.S.-1945

Subdivisional components remained a complete fiction.

135th Airborne Division-Phantom Division-Army of the U.S.-1945

Subdivisional components remained a complete fiction.

141st Infantry Division-Phantom Divsion-Army of the U.S.-1945

Subdivisional components remained a complete fiction.

157th Infantry Division-Phantom Division-Army of the U.S.-1945

Subdivisional components remained a complete fiction.

1954

1st Infantry Division-Active Component-Red One-1954

16th 18th 26th Infantry Regiments

5th 7th 32nd 33rd Field Artillery Battalions
48th Antiaircraft Artillery Battalion

63rd Tank Battalion

1st Signal Company
701st Ordnance Battalion
1st Quartermaster Company
1st Reconnaissance Company
1st Engineer Battalion
1st Medical Battalion
1st Military Police Company
1st Replacement Company

2nd Infantry Division-Active Component-Indianhead-1945

9th 23rd 38th Infantry Regiments

12th 15th 37th 38th Field Artillery Battalions
82nd Antiaircraft Artillery Battalion

72nd Tank Battalion

2nd Signal Company
702nd Ordnance Battalion
2nd Quartermaster Company
2nd Reconnaissance Company
2nd Engineer Battalion
2nd Medical Battalion
2nd military Police Company
2nd Replacement Company

3rd Infantry Division-Active Component-Marne-1945

7th 15th 30th Infantry Regiments

9th 10th 39th 41st Field Artillery Battalions
3rd Antiaircraft Artillery Battalion

64th Tank Battalion

3rd Signal Company
703rd Ordnance Battalion
3rd Quartermaster Company
3rd Reconnaissance Company
10th Engineer Battalion
3rd Medical Battalion
3rd Military Police Company
3rd Replacement Company

4th Infantry Division-Active Component-Ivy-1954

8th 12th 22nd Infantry Regiments

20th 29th 42nd 44th Field Artillery Battalions
46th Antiaircraft Artillery Battalion

40th Tank Battalion

4th Signal Company
704th Ordnance Battalion
4th Quartermaster Company
4th Reconnaissance Company
4th Engineer Battalion
4th Medical Battalion
4th Military Police Company
4th Replacement Company

5th Infantry Division-Active Component-Red Devils-1954

2nd 10th 11th Infantry Regiments

19th 21st 46th 50th Field Artillery Battalions
55th Antiaircraft Artillery Battalion

759th Tank Battalion

5th Signal Company
705th Ordnance Battalion
5th Quartermaster Company
5th Reconnaissance Company
7th Engineer Battalion
5th Medical Battalion
5th Military Police Company
5th Replacement Company

6th Infantry Division-Active Component-Red Star-1954

1st 20th 63rd Infantry Regiments

1st 51st 53rd 80th Field Artillery Battalions
6th Antiaircraft Artillery Battalion

92nd Tank Battalion

6th Signal Company
706th Ordnance Battalion
6th Quartermaster Company
6th Reconnaissance Company
6th Engineer Battalion
6th Medical Battalion
6th Military Police Company
6th Replacement Company

7th Infantry Division-Active Component-Bayonet-1954

17th 31st 32nd Infantry Regiments

31st 48th 49th 57th Field Artillery Battalions
15th Antiaircraft Artillery Battalion

73rd Tank Battalion

7th Signal Company
707th Ordnance Battalion
7th Quartermaster Company
7th Reconnaissance Company
13th Engineer Battalion
7th Medical Battalion
7th Military Police Company
7th Replacement Company

8th Infantry Division-Active Component-Pathfinders-1954

5th 13th 28th Infantry Regiments

28th 43rd 45th 56th Field Artillery Battalions
23rd Antiaircraft Artillery Battalion

41st Tank Battalion

8th Signal Company
708th Ordnance Battalion
8th Quartermaster Company
8th Reconnaissance Company
12th Engineer Battalion
8th Medical Battalion
8th Military Police Company
8th Replacement Company

9th Infantry Division-Active Component-Varsity-1954

39th 47th 60th Infantry Regiments

26th 34th 60th 84th Field Artillery Battalions
42nd Antiaircraft Artillery Battalion

61st Tank Battalion

9th Signal Company
709th Ordnance Battalion
9th Quartermaster Company
9th Reconnaissance Company
15th Engineer Battalion
9th Military Police Company
9th Replacement Company

10th Infantry Division-Active Component-Mountaineers-1954

85th 86th 87th Infantry Regiments

25th 35th 40th 85th Field Artillery Battalions
43rd Antiaircraft Artillery Battalion

62nd Tank Battalion

10th Signal Company
710th Ordnance Company
10th Quartermaster Company
10th Reconnaissance Company
41st Engineer Battalion
10th Medical Company
10th Military Police Company
10th Replacement Company

11th Airborne Division-Active Component-Angels-1954

188th 503rd 511th Infantry Regiments

89th 457th 544th 675th Field Artillery Battalions
88th Antiaircraft Artillery Battalion

76th 710th Tank Battalions

511th Signal Company
711th Ordnance Battalion
408th Quartermaster Company
127th Engineer Battalion
221st Medical Battalion
11th Military Police Company
11th Replacement Company

23rd Infantry Division-Active Component-Americal-1954

29th 33rd 65th Infantry Regiments

23rd 58th 219th 504th Field Artillery Battalions
276th Antiaircraft Artillery Battalion

714th Tank Battalion

123rd Signal Company
723rd Ordnance Battalion
23rd Quartermaster Company
23rd Reconnaissance Company
26th Engineer Battalion
23rd Medical Battalion
23rd Military Police Company
23rd Replacement Company

24th Infantry Division-Active Component-Victory-1954

19th 21st 34th Infantry Regiments

11th 13th 52nd 63rd Field Artillery Battalions
26th Antiaircraft Artillery Battalion

6th Tank Battalion

24th Signal Company
724th Ordnance Company
24th Quartermaster Company
24th Reconnaissance Company
3rd Engineer Battalion

24th Medical Battalion
24th Military Police Company
24th Replacement Company

25th Infantry Division-Active Component-Tropic Lightning-1954

14th 27th 35th Infantry Regiments

8th 64th 69th 90th Field Artillery Battalions
21st Antiaircraft Artillery Battalion

89th Tank Battalion

25th Signal Company
725th Ordnance Battalion
25th Quartermaster Company
25th Reconnaissance Company
65th Engineer Battalion
25th Medical Battalion
25th Military Police Company

26th Infantry Division-National Guard-Yankee-1954

101st 104th 181st Infantry Regiments

101st 102nd 180th 263rd Field Artillery Battalions
126th Antiaircraft Artillery Battalion

126th Tank Battalion

26th Signal Company
726th Ordnance Battalion
26th Quartermaster Company
26th Reconnaissance Company
101st Engineer Battalion
114th Medical Battalion
26th Military Police Company
26th Replacement Company

27th Infantry Division-National Guard-New York-1954

105th 108th 174th Infantry Regiments

106th 156th 170th 249th Field Artillery Battalions

127th Antiaircraft Artillery Battalion

127th Tank Battalion

27th Signal Company
727th Ordnance Battalion
27th Quartermaster Company
27th Reconnaissance Company
152nd Engineer Battalion
134th Medical Battalion
27th Military Police Company
27th Replacement Company

28th Infantry Division-National Guard-Keystone-1954

109th 110th 112th Infantry Regiments

107th 108th 109th 229th Field Artillery Battalions

899th Antiaircraft Artillery Battalion

628th Tank Battalion

28th Signal Company
728th Ordnance Company
28th Quartermaster Company
28th Reconnaissance Company
103rd Engineer Battalion
103rd Medical Battalion
28th Military Police Company
28th Replacement Company

29th Infantry Division-National Guard-Blue & Gray-1954
115th 116th 175th Infantry Regiments

110th 11th 224th 227th Field Artillery Battalions

129th Antiaircraft Artillery Battalion

197th Tank Battalion

29th Signal Company
729th Ordnance Battalion
29th Quartermaster Company
29th Reconnaissance Company
121st Engineer Battalion
104th Medical Battalion
29th Military Police Company
29th Replacement Company

30th Infantry Division-National Guard-Old Hickory-1954

119th 120th 139th Infantry Regiments

112th 113th 540th 690th Field Artillery Battalions

130th Antiaircraft Artillery Battalion

130th Tank Battalion

30th Signal Company
730th Ordnance Battalion
30th Quartermaster Company
30th Reconnaissance Company
105th Engineer Battalion
105th Medical Battalion
30th Military Police Company
30th Replacement Company

31st Infantry Division-National Guard-Dixie-1954

155th 167th 200th Infantry Regiments

114th 177th 932nd 933rd Field Artillery Battalions
104th Antiaircraft Artillery Battalion

198th Tank Battalion

31st Signal Company
731st Ordnance Company
31st Quartermaster Company
31st Reconnaissance Company
106th Engineer Battalion
106th Medical Battalion
31st Military Police Company
31st Replacement Company

32nd Infantry Division-National Guard-Red Arrow-1954

127th 128th 426th Infantry Regiments

120th 121st 126th 129th Field Artillery Battalions
132nd Antiaircraft Artillery Battalion

132nd Tank Battalion

32nd Signal Company
732nd Ordnance Company
32nd Quartermaster Company
32nd Reconnaissance Company
724th Engineer Battalion
135th Medical Battalion
32nd Military Police Company
32nd Replacement Company

33rd Infantry Division-National Guard-Prairie-1954

129th 130th 131st Infantry Regiments

122nd 123rd 124th 210th Field Artillery Battalions
133rd Antiaircraft Artillery Battalion

106th Tank Battalion

33rd Signal Company
733rd Ordnance Company
33rd Quartermaster Company
33rd Reconnaissance Company
108th Engineer Battalion
108th Medical Battalion
33rd Military Police Company
33rd Replacement Company

34th Infantry Division-National Guard-Red Bull-1954

133rd 134th 168th Infantry Regiments

185th 194th 554th 556th Field Artillery Battalions113th Antiaircraft Artillery Battalion

195th Tank Battalion

34th Signal Company
734th Ordnance Battalion
34th Quartermaster Company
34th Reconnaissance Company
128th Engineer Battalion
109th Medical Battalion
34th Military Police Company
34th Replacement Company

35th Infantry Division-National Guard-Santa Fe-1954

137th 138th 140th Infantry Regiments

127th 128th 129th 154th Field Artillery Battalions
135th Antiaircraft Artillery Battalion

135th Tank Battalion

35th Signal Company
735th Ordnance Company
35th Quartermaster Company
35th Reconnaissance Company
110th Engineer Battalion
205th Medical Battalion
35th Military Police Company
35th Replacement Company

36th Infantry Division-National Guard-Texas-1954

141st 142nd 143rd Infantry Regiments

131st 132nd 133rd 155th Field Artillery Battalions
136th Antiaircraft Artillery Battalion

136th Tank Battalion

36th Signal Company
736th Ordnance Battalion
36th Quartermaster Company
36th Reconnaissance Company
111th Engineer Battalion
111th Medical Battalion
36th Military Police Company
36th Replacement Company

37th Infantry Division-National Guard-Buckeye-1954

145th 147th 148th Infantry Regiments

134th 135th 136th 140th Field Artillery Battalions
137th Antiaircraft Artillery Battalion

137th Tank Battalion

37th Signal Company
737th Ordnance Company
37th Quartermaster Company
37th Reconnaissance Company

112th Engineer Battalion
112th Medical Battalion
37th Military Police Company
37th Replacement Company

38th Infantry Division-National Guard-Cyclone-1954

151st 152nd 293rd Infantry Regiments

139th 150th 163rd 524th Field Artillery Battalions
138th Antiaircraft Artillery Battalion

138th Tank Battalion

38th Signal Company
738th Ordnance Battalion
38th Quartermaster Company
38th Reconnaissance Company
113th Engineer Battalion
113th Medical Battalion
38th Military Police Company
38th Replacement Company

39th Infantry Division-National Guard-Delta-1954

153rd 156th 199th Infantry Regiments

141st 437th 445th 937th Field Artillery Battalions
105th Antiaircraft Artillery Battalion

206th Tank Battalion

39th Signal Company
739th Ordnance Battalion
39th Quartermaster Company
39th Reconnaissance Company
217th Engineer Battalion
125th Medical Battalion
39th Military Police Company
39th Replacement Company

40th Infantry Division-National Guard-Sunrise-1954

160th 223rd 224th Infantry Regiments

143rd 164th 980th 981st Field Artillery Battalions
140th Antiaircraft Artillery Battalion

140th Tank Battalion

40th Signal Company
740th Ordnance Battalion
40th Quartermaster Company
40th Reconnaissance Company
575th Engineer Battalion
115th Medical Battalion
40th Military Police Company
40th Replacement Company

41st Infantry Division-National Guard-Sunset-1954

161st 162nd 186th Infantry Regiments

146th 147th 218th 965th Field Artillery Battalions
700th Antiaircraft Artillery Battalion

803rd Tank Battalion

41st Signal Company
741st Ordnance Battalion
41st Quartermaster Company
41st Reconnaissance Company
162nd Engineer Battalion
116th Medical Battalion
41st Military Police Company
41st Replacement Company

42nd Infantry Division-National Guard-Rainbow-1954

71st 106th 165th Infantry Regiments

104th 106th 226th 258th Field Artillery Battalions

142nd Antiaircraft Artillery Battalion

142nd Tank Battalion

42nd Signal Company
742nd Ordnance Battalion
42nd Quartermaster Company
42nd Reconnaissance Company
102nd Engineer Battalion
102nd Medical Battalion
42nd Military Police Company
42nd Replacement Company

43rd Infantry Division-National Guard-Red Wing-1954

102nd 169th 172nd Infantry Regiments

102nd 192nd 206th 963rd Field Artillery Battalions
169th Antiaircraft Artillery Battalion

143rd Tank Battalion

43rd Signal Company
743rd Ordnance Battalion
43rd Quartermaster Company
43rd Reconnaissance Company
118th Engineer Battalion
118th Medical Battalion
43rd Military Police Company
43rd Replacement Company

44th Infantry Division-National Guard-1954

123rd 129th 130th Infantry Regiments

123rd 209th 223rd 233rd Field Artillery Battalions
144th Antiaircraft Artillery Battalion

106th Tank Battalion

44th Signal Company
744th Ordnance Battalion
44th Quartermaster Company
44th Reconnaissance Company
135th Engineer Battalion
203rd Medical Battalion
44th Military Police Company
44th Replacement Company

45th Infantry Division-National Guard-Thunderbirds-1954

179th 180th 279th Infantry Regiments

158th 160th 171st 189th Field Artillery Battalions
145th Antiaircraft Artillery Battalion

245th Tank Battalion
45th Signal Company
700th Ordnance Battalion
45th Quartermaster Company
45th Reconnaissance Company
120th Engineer Battalion
120th Medical Battalion
45th Military Police Company
45th Replacement Company

45th Infantry Division-National Guard-Thunderbirds-1954

179th 180th 279th Infantry Regiments

158th 160th 171st 189th Field Artillery Battalions
145th Antiaircraft Artillery Battalion

245th Tank Battalion

45th Signal Company
700th Ordnance Battalion
45th Quartermaster Company
45th Reconnaissance Company
120th Engineer Battalion

120th Medical Battalion
45th Military Police Company
45th Replacement Company

46th Infantry Division-National Guard-Ironfist-1954

125th 126th 425th Infantry Regiments

119th 177th 182nd 943rd Field Artillery Battalions
146th Antiaircraft Artillery Battalion

246th Tank Battalion

46th Signal Company
746th Ordnance Battalion
46th Quartermaster Company
46th Reconnaissance Company
107th Engineer Battalion
107th Medical Battalion
46th Military Police Company
46th Replacement Company

47th Infantry Division-National Guard-Viking-1954

135th 136th 164th Infantry Regiments

125th 151st 175th 185th Field Artillery Battalions
256th Antiaircraft Artillery Battalion

194th Tank Battalion

47th Signal Company
747th Ordnance Battalion
47th Quartermaster Company
47th Reconnaissance Company
682nd Engineer Battalion
204th Medical Battalion
47th Military Police Company
47th Replacement Company

48th Infantry Division-National Guard-Hurricane-1954

121st 122nd 124th Infantry Regiments

118th 149th 179th 230th Field Artillery Battalions
148th Antiaircraft Artillery Battalion

190th Tank Battalion

48th Signal Company
748th Ordnance Battalion
48th Quartermaster Company
48th Reconnaissance Company
560th Engineer Battalion
202nd Medical Battalion
48th Military Police Company
48th Replacement Company

49th Infantry Division-National Guard-Argonaunt-1954

159th 184th 185th Infantry Regiments

164th 629th 636th 637th Field Artillery Battalions
149th Antiaircraft Artillery Battalion

149th Tank Battalion

49th Signal Company
749th Ordnance Battalion
49th Quartermaster Company
49th Reconnaissance Company
579th Engineer Battalion
126th Medical Battalion
49th Military Police Company
49th Replacement Company

51st Infantry Division-National Guard-Rattlesnake-1954

118th 211th 218th Infantry Regiments

116th 178th 248th 296th Field Artillery Battalions
107th Antiaircraft Artillery Battalion

263rd Tank Battalion

51st Signal Company
751st Ordnance Company
51st Quartermaster Company
51st Reconnaissance Company
122nd Engineer Battalion
201st Medical Battalion
51st Military Police Company
51st Replacement Company

63rd Infantry Division-Army Reserve-Blood & Fire-1954

253rd 254th 255th Infantry Regiments

718th 863rd 864th 865th Field Artillery Battalions
574th Antiaircraft Artillery Battalion

350th Tank Battalion

63rd Signal Company
763rd Ordnance Battalion
63rd Quartermaster Company
63rd Reconnaissance Company
263rd Engineer Battalion
363rd Medical Battalion
63rd Military Police Company
63rd Replacement Company

69th Infantry Division-Active Component-Fighting 69th-1954

271st 272nd 273rd Infantry Regiments

724th 879th 880th 881st Field Artillery Battalions
474th Antiaircraft Artillery Battalion

893rd Tank Battalion

569th Signal Company
769th Ordnance Battalion
69th Quartermaster Company
69th Reconnaissance Company
269th Engineer Battalion
369th Medical Battalion
69th Military Police Company
69th Replacement Company

70th Infantry Division-Army Reserve-Trailblazer-1954

329th 330th 333rd Infantry Regiments

325th 745th 882nd 883rd Field Artillery Battalions
385th Antiaircraft Artillery Battalion

703rd Tank Battalion

570th Signal Company
770th Ordnance Battalion
70th Quartermaster Company
70th Reconnaissance Company
270th Engineer Battalion
370th Medical Battalion
70th Military Police Company
70th Replacement Company

71st Infantry Division-Active Component-Red Circle-1954

4th 5th 53rd Infantry Regiments

274th 555th 564th 607th Field Artillery Battalions
167th Antiaircraft Artillery Battalion

723rd Tank Battalion

571st Signal Company
771st Ordnance Company
71st Quartermaster Company
271st Engineer Battalion
371st Medical Battalion
71st Military Police Company
71st Replacement Company

75th Infantry Division-Army Reserve-1954

289th 290th 377th Infantry Regiments

345th 897th 898th 899th Field Artillery Battalions
440th Antiaircraft Artillery Battalion744th Tank Battalion

575th Signal Company
775th Ordnance Battalion
75th Quartermaster Company
75th Reconnaissance Company
275th Engineer Battalion
375th Medical Battalion
75th Military Police Company
75th Replacement Company

76th Infantry Division-Army Resreve-Onaway-1954

304th 385th 417th Infantry Regiments

302nd 355th 364th 901st Field Artillery Battalions
461st Antiaircraft Artillery Battalion

740th Tank Battalion

76th Signal Company
776th Ordnance Battalion

76th Quartermaster Company
76th Reconnaissance Company
301st Engineer Battalion
301st Medical Battalion
76th Military Police Company
76th Replacement Company

77th Infantry Division-Army Reserve-Statue of Liberty-1954

305th 306th 307th Infantry Regiments

304th 305th 306th 902nd Field Artillery Battalions
469th Antiaircraft Artillery Battalion

819th Tank Battalion

77th Signal Company
777th Ordnance Battalion
77th Quartermaster Company
77th Reconnaissance Company
302nd Engineer Battalion
302nd Medical Battalion
77th Military Police Company
77th Replacement Company

78th Infantry Division-Army Reserve-Lightning-1954

309th 310th 311th Infantry Regiments

307th 308th 309th 903rd Field Artillery Battalions
430th Antiaircraft Artillery Battalion

766th Tank Battalion

78th Signal Company
778th Ordnance Battalion
78th Quartermaster Company
78th Reconnaissance Company
303rd Engineer Battalion
303rd Medical Battalion

78th Military Police Company
78th Replacement Company

79th Infantry Division-Army Reserve-Cross of Lorriane-1954

313th 314th 315th Infantry Regiments

310th 311th 312th 904th Field Artillery Battalions
463rd Antiaircraft Artillery Battalion

813th Tank Battalion

79th Signal Company
779th Ordnance Battalion
79th Quartermaster Company
79th Reconnaissance Company
304th Engineer Battalion
304th Medical Battalion
79th Military Police Company
79th Replacement Company

79th Infantry Division-Army Reserve-Cross of Lorriane-1954

313th 314th 315th Infantry Regiments

310th 311th 312th 904th Field Artillery Battalions
463rd Antiaircraft Artillery Battalion

813th Tank Battalion

79th Signal Company
779th Ordnance Battalion
79th Quartermaster Company
79th Reconnaissance Company
304th Engineer Battalion
304th Medical Battalion
79th Military Police Company
79th Replacement Company

80th Infantry Division-Army Reserve-Blue Ridge-1954

317th 318th 319th Infantry Regiments

313th 314th 315th 905th Field Artillery Battalions
486th Antiaircraft Artillery Battalion

610th Tank Battalion

80th Signal Company
780th Ordnance Battalion
80th Quartermaster Company
80th Reconnaissance Company
305th Engineer Battalion
305th Medical Battalion
80th Military Police Company
80th Replacement Company

81st Infantry Division-Army Reserve-Wildcat-1954

322nd 345th 519th Infantry Regiments

257th 317th 334th 507th Field Artillery Battalions
325th Antiaircraft Artillery Battalion

726th Tank Battalion

81st Signal Company
781st Ordnance Battalion
81st Quartermaster Company
81st Reconnaissance Company
306th Engineer Battalion
306th Medical Battalion
81st Military Police Company
81st Replacement Company

82nd Airborne Division-Active Component-All American-1954

325th 504th 505th Infantry Regiments

89th 319th 376th 456th Field Artillery Battalions
80th Antiaircraft Artillery Battalion

44th 714th Tank Battalions

82nd Signal Company
782nd Ordnance Battalion
407th Quartermaster Company
82nd Reconnaissance Company
307th Engineer Battalion
307th Medical Battalion
82nd Military Police Company
82nd Replacement Company

83rd Infantry Division-Army Reserve-Thunderbolt-1954

331st 332nd 336th Infantry Regiments

322nd 323rd 324th 908th Field Artillery Battalions
453rd Antiaircraft Artillery Battalion

778th Tank Battalion

83rd Signal Company783rd Ordnance Battalion
83rd Quartermaster Company
83rd Reconnaissance Company
398th Engineer Battalion
308th Medical Battalion
83rd Military Police Company
83rd Replacement Company

83rd Infantry Division-Army Reserve-Thunderbolt-1954

331st 332nd 336th Infantry Regiments

322nd 323rd 324th 908th Field Artillery Battalions

453rd Antiaircraft Artillery Battalion

778th Tank Battalion

83rd Signal Company
783rd Ordnance Battalion
83rd Quartermaster Company
83rd Reconnaissance Company
398th Engineer Battalion
308th Medical Battalion
83rd Military Police Company
83rd Replacement Company

84th Infantry Division-Army Reserve-Railsplitters-1954

274th 334th 339th Infantry Regiments

326th 327th 884th 909th Field Artillery Battalions
557th Antiaircraft Artillery Battalion

808th Tank Battalion

84th Signal Company
784th Ordnance Battalion
84th Quartermaster Company
84th Reconnaissance Company
309th Engineer Battalion
309th Medical Battalion
84th Military Police Company
84th Replacement Company

85th Infantry Division-Army Reserve-Custer-1954

335th 337th 338th Infantry Regiments

328th 403rd 725th 910th Field Artillery Battalions
134th Antiaircraft Artillery Battalion

749th Tank Battalion

85th Signal Company
785th Ordnance Battalion
85th Quartermaster Company
85th Reconnaissance Company
310th Engineer Battalion
310th Medical Battalion
85th Military Police Company
85th Replacement Company

87th Infantry Division-Army Reserve-Acorn-1954

346th 347th 485th Infantry Regiments

335th 336th 581st 582nd Field Artillery Battalions
487th Antiaircraft Artillery Battalion

812th Tank Battalion

87th Signal Company
787th Ordnance Battalion
87th Quartermaster Company
87th Reconnaissance Company
312th Engineer Battalion
312th Medical Battalion
87th Military Police Company
87th Replacement Company

89th Infantry Division-Army Reserve-Rolling W-1954

353rd 354th 355th Infantry Regiments

340th 341st 342nd 563rd Field Artillery Battalions
489th Antiaircraft Artillery Battalion

389th Tank Battalion

89th Signal Company
789th Ordnance Battalion
89th Quartermaster Company
89th Reconnaissance Company

314th Engineer Battalion
314th Medical Battalion
89th Military police Company
89th Replacement Company

90th Infantry Division-Army Reserve-Tough Ombres-1954

357th 358th 359th Infantry Regiments

343rd 344th 730th 915th Field Artillery Battalions
537th Antiaircraft Artillery Battalion

737th Tank Battalion

90th Signal Company
790th Ordnance Battalion
90th Quartermaster Company
90th Reconnaissance Company
315th Engineer Battalion
315th Medical Battalion
90th Military Police Company
90th Replacement Company

91st Infantry Division-Army Reserve-Powder River-1954

361st 362nd 363rd Infantry Regiments

346th 347th 348th 916th Field Artillery Battalions
491st Antiaircraft Artillery Battalion

767th Tank Battalion

91st Signal Company
791st Ordnance Battalion
91st Quartermaster Company
91st Reconnaissance Company
316th Engineer Battalion
316th Medical Battalion
91st Military Police Company
91st Replacement Company

94th Infantry Division-Army Reserve-Nuef Quartes-1954

301st 302nd 376th Infantry Regiments

301st 356th 390th 919th Field Artillery Battalions
494th Antiaircraft Artillery Battalion

762nd Tank Battalion

94th Signal Company
794th Ordnance Battalion
94th Quartermaster Company
94th Reconnaissance Company
319th Engineer Battalion
319th Medical Battalion
94th Military Police Company
94th Replacement Company

95th Infantry Division-Army Reserve-Iron Men of Metz-1954

291st 378th 379th Infantry Regiments

358th 359th 360th 920th Field Artillery Battalions
391st Antiaircraft Artillery Battalion

735th Tank Battalion

95th Signal Company
795th Ordnance Battalion
95th Quartermaster Company
95th Reconnaissance Company
320th Engineer Battalion
320th Medical Battalion
95th Military Police Company
95th Replacement Company

96th Infantry Division-Army Reserve-Deadeyes-1954

59th 381st 383rd Infantry Regiments

361st 362nd 498th 921st Field Artillery Battalions
785th Antiaircraft Artillery Battalion

24th Tank Battalion

96th Signal Company
796th Ordnance Battalion
96th Quartermaster Company
96th Reconnaissance Company
321st Engineer Battalion
321st Medical Battalion
96th Military police Company
96th Replacement Company

98th Infantry Division-Army Reserve-Iroquois-1954

389th 390th 391st Infantry Regiments

367th 368th 369th 923rd Field Artillery Battalions
400th Antiaircraft Artillery Battalion

817th Tank Battalion

98th Signal Company
798th Ordnance Battalion
98th Quartermaster Company
98th Reconnaissance Company
323rd Engineer Battalion
323rd Medical Battalion
98th Military Police Company
98th Replacement Company

100th Infantry Division-Army Reserve-Century-1954

397th 398th 399th Infantry Regiments

373rd 374th 375th 925th Field Artillery Battalions
482nd Antiaircraft Artillery Battalion

824th Tank Battalion

100th Signal Company
800th Ordnance Battalion
100th Quartermaster Company
100th Reconnaissance Company
325th Engineer Battalion
325th Medical Battalion
100th Military Police Company
100th Replacement Company

101st Airborne Division-Active Component-Screaming Eagles-1954

501st 502nd 506th Infantry Regiments

81st 515th 516th 518th Field Artillery Battalion
81st Antiaircraft Artillery Battalion

42nd 65th Tank Battalions

101st Signal Company
801st Ordnance Battalion
426th Quartermaster Company
101st Reconnaissance Company
326th Engineer Battalion
326th Medical Battalion
101st Military Police Company
101st Replacement Company

102nd Infantry Division-Army Reserve-Ozark-1954

405th 406th 407th Infantry Regiments

379th 380th 381st 927th Field Artillery Battalions454[th] Antiaircraft Artillery Battalion

705th Tank Battalion

102nd Signal Company
802nd Ordnance Battalion
102nd Quartermaster Company
102nd Reconnaissance Company
327th Engineer Battalion
327th Medical Battalion
102nd military Police Company
102nd Replacement Company

103rd Infantry Division-Army Reserve-Catcus-1954

409th 410th 411th Infantry Regiments

382nd 383rd 384th 928th Field Artillery Battalions
438th Antiaircraft Artillery Battalion

781st Tank Battalion

103rd Signal Company
803rd Ordnance Battalion
103rd Quartermaster Company
103rd Reconnaissance Company
328th Engineer Battalion
328th Medical Battalion
103rd Military Police Company
103rd Replacement Company
104th Infantry Division-Army Reserve-Timberwolves-1954

413th 414th 415th Infantry Regiments

385th 386th 387th 929th Field Artillery Battalions
555th Antiaircraft Artillery Battalion

718th Tank Battalion

104th Signal Company
804th Ordnance Battalion

104th Quartermaster Company
104th Reconnaissance Company
329th Engineer Battalion
329th Medical Battalion
104th Military Police Company
104th Replacement Company

108th Infantry Division-Army Reserve-Golden Griffon-1954

321st 323rd 518th Infantry Regiments

316th 318th 506th 906th Field Artillery Battalions
481st Antiaircraft Artillery Battalion

602nd Tank Battalion

108th Signal Company
808th Ordnance Battalion
108th Quartermaster Company
108th Reconnaissance Company
598th Engineer Battalion
353rd Medical Battalion
108th Military Police Company
108th Replacement Company

1960

1st Infantry Division-Active Component-Big Red One-1960

1st Battle Group 5th Infantry
2nd Battle Group 8th Infantry
2nd Battle Group 12th Infantry
1st Battle Group 13th Infantry
1st Battle Group 28th Infantry

8th Battalion 4th Artillery
1st Battalion 5th Artillery
8th Battalion 6th Artillery
1st Battalion 7th Artillery
5th Battalion 32nd Artillery
2nd Battalion 33rd Artillery

1st Battalion 69th Armor

1st Squadron 4th Cavalry

701st Ordnance Battalion
1st Engineer Battalion
1st Medical Battalion
121st Signal Battalion
9th Transportation Battalion
1st Aviation Company
1st Administration Company
1st Aircraft Maintenance Detachment

2nd Infantry Division-Active Component-Indianhead-1960

2nd Battle Group 1st Infantry
2nd Battle Group 9th Infantry
1st Battle Group 11th Infantry
2nd Battle Group 23rd Infantry
1st Battle Group 87th Infantry

1st Battalion 12th Artillery
1st Battalion 15th Artillery
7th Battalion 17th Artillery
1st Battalion 27th Artillery
6th Battalion 37th Artillery
5th Battalion 38th Artillery

2nd Battalion 69th Armor

3rd Squadron 7th Cavalry

702nd Ordnance Battalion
2nd Engineer Battalion
2nd Medical Battalion
122nd Signal Battalion
13th Transportation Battalion
2nd Quartermaster Company
2nd Aviation Company
2nd Administration Company
2nd Aircraft Maintenance Detachment

3rd Infantry Division-Active Component-Marne-1960

2nd Battle Group 4th Infantry
1st Battle Group 7th Infantry
1st Battle Group 15th Infantry
1st Battle Group 30th Infantry
2nd Battle Group 38th Infantry

1st Battalion 9th Artillery
1st Battalion 10th Artillery
6th Battalion 18th Artillery
2nd Battalion 39th Artillery
2nd Battalion 41st Artillery
3rd Battalion 76th Artillery

1st Battalion 68th Armor

2nd Squadron 7th Cavalry

703rd Ordnance Battalion

10th Engineer Battalion
3rd Medical Battalion
123rd Signal Battalion
35th Transportation Battalion
3rd Quartermaster Company
3rd Aviation Company
3rd Administration Company
3rd Aircraft Maintenance Detachment

4th Infantry Division-Active Component-Ivy-1960

1st Battle Group 8th Infantry
1st Battle Group 12th Infantry
1st Battle Group 22nd Infantry
2nd Battle Group 39th Infantry
2nd Battle Group 47th Infantry

2nd Battalion 1st Artillery
5th Battalion 16th Artillery
1st Battalion 20th Artillery
6th Battalion 29th Artillery
4th Battalion 42nd Artillery
2nd Battalion 77th Artillery

1st Battalion 34th Armor

2nd Squadron 8th Cavalry

704th Ordnance Battalion
4th Engineer Battalion
4th Medical Battalion
124th Signal Battalion
14th Transportation Battalion
4th Quartermaster Company
4th Aviation Company
4th Administration Company
4th Aircraft Maintenance Detachment

7th Infantry Division-Active Component-Bayonet-1960

2nd Battle Group 3rd Infantry
1st Battle Group 17th Infantry
1st Battle Group 31st Infantry
1st Battle Group 32nd Infantry
2nd Battle Group 34th Infantry

2nd Battalion 8th Artillery
6th Battalion 15th Artillery
1st Battalion 31st Artillery
4th Battalion 76th Artillery
1st Battalion 79th Artillery
6th Battalion 80th Artillery

2nd Battalion 40th Armor

2nd Squadron 10th Cavalry

707th Ordnance Battalion
13th Engineer Battalion
7th Medical Battalion
127th Signal Battalion
17th Transportation Battalion
7th Quartermaster Company
7th Aviation Company
7th Administration Company
7th Aircraft Maintenance Detachment

8th Infantry Division-Active Component-Pathfinders-1960

1st Battle Group 16th Infantry
1st Battle Group 18th Infantry
1st Battle Group 26th Infantry
1st Airborne Battle Group 504th Infantry
1st Airborne Battle Group 505th Infantry

1st Battalion 2nd Artillery
2nd Battalion 12th Artillery
7th Battalion 16th Artillery
1st Battalion 28th Artillery

5th Battalion 81st Artillery
5th Battalion 83rd Artillery

2nd Battalion 68th Armor

3rd Squadron 8th Cavalry

708th Ordnance Battalion
12th Engineer Battalion
8th Medical Battalion
128th Signal Battalion
20th Transportation Battalion
8th Quartermaster Company
8th Aviation Company
8th Administration Company
8th Aircraft Maintenance Detachment

9th Infantry Division-Active Component-Old Reliables-1960

2nd Battle Group 5th Infantry
2nd Battle Group 13th Infantry
1st Battle Group 39th Infantry
1st Battle Group 47th Infantry
1st Battle Group 60th Infantry

2nd Battalion 4th Artillery
1st Battalion 11th Artillery

3rd Battalion 68th Armor

3rd Squadron 5th Cavalry

709th Ordnance Battalion
15th Engineer Battalion
9th Medical Battalion
9th Signal Battalion
22nd Transportation Battalion
9th Quartermaster Company
9th Aviation Company
9th Administration Company
9th Aircraft Maintenance Detachment

10th Infantry Division-Active Component-Mountaineers-1957

2nd Battle Group 7th Infantry
2nd Battle Group 10th Infantry
2nd Battle Group 15th Infantry
2nd Battle Group 29th Infantry
1st Battle Group 87th Infantry

2nd Battalion 7th Artillery
2nd Battalion 9th Artillery

2nd Battalion 69th Armor

3rd Squadron 7th Cavalry

710th Ordnance Battalion
41st Engineer Battalion
10th Medical Battalion
110th Signal Battalion
30th Transportation Battalion
10th Quartermaster Company
10th Aviation Company
10th Administration Company
10th Aircraft Maintenance Detachment

11th Airborne Division-Active Component-Angels-1957

1st Airborne Battle Group 187th Infantry
2nd Airborne Battle Group 502nd Infantry
1st Airborne Battle Group 503rd Infantry
2nd Airborne Battle Group 504th Infantry
2nd Airborne Battle Group 505th Infantry

Battery A 320th Artillery
Battery B 320th Artillery
Battery C 320th Artillery
Battery D 321st Artillery
Battery E 321st Artillery
Battery C 377th Artillery

Troop C 17th Cavalry

711th Ordnance Battalion
127th Engineer Battalion
11th Medical Battalion
511th Signal Battalion
11th Transportation Battalion
408th Quartermaster Company
11th Aviation Company
11th Administration Company
11th Aircraft Maintenance Detachment

24th Infantry Division-Active Component-Victory-1960

2nd Battle Group 2nd Infantry
1st Battle Group 19th Infantry
1st Battle Group 21st Infantry
2nd Battle Group 28th Infantry
1st Battle Group 34th Infantry

2nd Battalion 7th Artillery
3rd Battalion 11th Artillery
1st Battalion 13th Artillery
1st Battalion 34th Artillery
1st Battalion 35th Artillery
5th Battalion 92nd Artillery

3rd Battalion 34th Armor

2nd Squadron 9th Cavalry

724th Ordnance Battalion
3rd Engineer Battalion
24th Medical Battalion
24th Signal Battalion
31st Transportation Battalion
24th Quartermaster Company
24th Aviation Company
24th Administration Company
24th Aircraft Maintenance Detachment

25th Infantry Division-Active Component-Tropic Lightning-1960

1st Battle Group 14th Infantry
2nd Battle Group 19th Infantry
2nd Battle Group 21st Infantry
1st Battle Group 27th Infantry
1st Battle Group 34th Infantry

9th Battalion 1st Artillery
1st Battalion 8th Artillery
2nd Battalion 9th Artillery
7th Battalion 11th Artillery
3rd Battalion 13th Artillery
2nd Battalion 21st Artillery

3rd Battalion 69th Armor

3rd Squadron 4th Cavalry

725th Ordnance Battalion
65th Engineer Battalion
25th Medical Battalion
125th Signal Battalion
33rd Transportation Battalion
25th Quartermaster Company
25th Aviation Company
25th Administration Company
25th Aircraft Maintenance Detachment

26th Infantry Division-National Guard-Yankee-1960

1st Battle Group 101st Infantry
1st Battle Group 104th Infantry
1st Battle Group 181st Infantry
1st Battle Group 182nd Infantry
1st Battle Group 220th Infantry

1st Battalion 101st Artillery
2nd Battalion 101st Artillery
3rd Battalion 101st Artillery
1st Battalion 102nd Artillery
2nd Battalion 102nd Artillery

3rd Battalion 102nd Artillery

1st Battalion 110th Armor

2nd Squadron 110th Armor

726th Ordnance Battalion
114th Engineer Battalion
101st Medical Battalion
126th Signal Battalion
226th Transportation Battalion
26th Quartermaster Company
26th Aviation Company
26th Administration Company
226th Aircraft Maintenance Detachment

28th Infantry Division-National Guard-Keystone-1960

1st Battle Group 109th Infantry
1st Battle Group 110th Infantry
1st Battle Group 111th Infantry
2nd Battle Group 111th Infantry
1st Battle Group 112th Infantry

1st Battalion 107th Artillery
1st Battalion 108th Artillery
1st Battalion 109th Artillery
2nd Battalion 109th Artillery
1st Battalion 166th Artillery
1st Battalion 229th Artillery

2nd Battalion 103rd Armor

1st Squadron 103rd Armor

728th Ordnance Battalion
103rd Engineer Battalion
103rd Medical Battalion
28th Signal Battalion
228th Transportation Battalion
28th Quartermaster Company

28th Aviation Company
28th Administration Company
228th Aircraft Maintenance Detachment

29th Infantry Division-National Guard-Blue & Gray-1960

1st Battle Group 115th Infantry
2nd Battle Group 115th Infantry
1st Battle Group 116th Infantry
2nd Battle Group 116th Infantry
1st Battle Group 175th Infantry

1st Battalion 110th Artillery
2nd Battalion 110th Artillery
3rd Battalion 110th Artillery
1st Battalion 111th Artillery
1st Battalion 246th Artillery
2nd Battalion 246th Artillery

1st Battalion 115th Armor

1st Squadron 183rd Armor

729th Ordnance Battalion
121st Engineer Battalion
104th Medical Battalion
129th Signal Battalion
229th Transportation Battalion
29th Quartermaster Company
29th Aviation Company
29th Administration Company
29th Aircraft Maintenance Detachment

30th Infantry Division-National Guard-Old Hickory-1960

1st Battle Group 119th Infantry
2nd Battle Group 119th Infantry
1st Battle Group 120th Infantry
2nd Battle Group 120th Infantry
3rd Battle Group 120th Infantry

1st Battalion 113th Artillery
2nd Battalion 113th Artillery
3rd Battalion 113th Artillery
4th Battalion 113th Artillery
5th Battalion 113th Artillery
1st Battalion 252nd Artillery

1st Battalion 196th Armor

2nd Squadron 196th Armor

730th Ordnance Battalion
105th Engineer Battalion
105th Medical Battalion
130th Signal Battalion
230th Transportation Battalion
30th Quartermaster Company
30th Aviation Company
30th Administration Company
230th Aircraft Maintenance Detachment

31st Infantry Division-National Guard-Dixie-1960

1st Battle Group 155th Infantry
2nd Battle Group 155th Infantry
1st Battle Group 167th Infantry
2nd Battle Group 167th Infantry
1st Battle Group 200th Infantry

1st Battalion 114th Artillery
2nd Battalion 114th Artillery
3rd Battalion 114th Artillery
1st Battalion 117th Artillery
2nd Battalion 117th Artillery
1st Battalion 203rd Artillery

1st Battalion 198th Armor

2nd Squadron 198th Armor

731st Ordnance Battalion
106th Engineer Battalion
106th Medical Battalion
131st Signal Battalion
131st Transportation Battalion
31st Quartermaster Company
31st Aviation Company
31st Administration Company
31st Aircraft Maintenance Detachment

32nd Infantry Division-National Guard-Red Arrow-1960

1st Battle Group 127th Infantry
2nd Battle Group 127th Infantry
3rd Battle Group 127th Infantry
1st Battle Group 128th Infantry
2nd Battle Group 128th Infantry

1st Battalion 120th Artillery
2nd Battalion 120th Artillery
1st Battalion 121st Artillery
2nd Battalion 121st Artillery
1st Battalion 126th Artillery
2nd Battalion 126th Artillery

1st Battalion 105th Armor

2nd Squadron 105th Armor

732nd Ordnance Battalion
724th Engineer Battalion
135th Medical Battalion
132nd Signal Battalion
232nd Transportation Battalion
32nd Quartermaster Company
32nd Aviation Company
32nd Administration Company
232nd Aircraft Maintenance Detachment

33rd Infantry Division-National Guard-Prairie-1960

1st Battle Group 129th Infantry
2nd Battle Group 129th Infantry
1st Battle Group 130th Infantry
2nd Battle Group 130th Infantry
1st Battle Group 131st Infantry

1st Battalion 122nd Artillery
2nd Battalion 122nd Artillery
3rd Battalion 122nd Artillery
4th Battalion 122nd Artillery
1st Battalion 123rd Artillery
2nd Battalion 123rd Artillery

1st Battalion 106th Armor

2nd Squadron 106th Armor

733rd Ordnance Battalion
108th Engineer Battalion
108th Medical Battalion
133rd Signal Battalion
108th Transportation Battalion
33rd Quartermaster Company
33rd Aviation Company
33rd Administration Company
33rd Aircraft Maintenance Detachment

34th Infantry Division-National Guard-Red Bull-1960

1st Battle Group 133rd Infantry
2nd Battle Group 133rd Infantry
1st Battle Group 134th Infantry
2nd Battle Group 134th Infantry
1st Battle Group 168th Infantry

1st Battalion 168th Artillery
2nd Battalion 168th Artillery
1st Battalion 185th Artillery
2nd Battalion 185th Artillery

3rd Battalion 185th Artillery
4th Battalion 185th Artillery

1st Battalion 113th Armor

2nd Squadron 113th Armor

734th Ordnance Battalion
128th Engineer Battalion
109th Medical Battalion
234th Signal Battalion
234th Transportation Battalion
34th Quartermaster Company
34th Aviation Company
34th Administration Company
34th Aircraft Maintenance Detachment

35th Infantry Division-National Guard-Santa Fe-1960

1st Battle Group 137th Infantry
2nd Battle Group 137th Infantry
1st Battle Group 138th Infantry
2nd Battle Group 138th Infantry
1st Battle Group 140th Infantry

1st Battalion 127th Artillery
1st Battalion 128th Artillery
2nd Battalion 128th Artillery
1st Battalion 129th Artillery
2nd Battalion 130th Artillery
1st Battalion 235th Artillery

1st Battalion 203rd Armor

2nd Squadron 203rd Armor

735th Ordnance Battalion
110th Engineer Battalion
205th Medical Battalion
135th Signal Battalion
135th Transportation Battalion
35th Quartermaster Company

35th Aviation Company
35th Administration Company
35th Aircraft Maintenance Detachment

36th Infantry Division-National Guard-Texas-1960

1st Battle Group 141st Infantry
1st Battle Group 142nd Infantry
2nd Battle Group 142nd Infantry
1st Battle Group 143rd Infantry
2nd Battle Group 143rd Infantry

1st Battalion 131st Artillery
1st Battalion 133rd Artillery
2nd Battalion 133rd Artillery
3rd Battalion 133rd Artillery
4th Battalion 133rd Artillery
5th Battalion 133rd Artillery

1st Battalion 124th Armor

2nd Squadron 124th Armor

736th Ordnance Battalion
111th Engineer Battalion
111th Medical Battalion
136th Signal Battalion
111th Transportation Battalion
36th Quartermaster Company
36th Aviation Company
36th Administration Company
36th Aircraft Maintenance Detachment

37th Infantry Division-National Guard-Buckeye-1960

1st Battle Group 145th Infantry
1st Battle Group 147th Infantry
1st Battle Group 148th Infantry
2nd Battle Group 148th Infantry
1st Battle Group 166th Infantry

1st Battalion 134th Artillery
2nd Battalion 134th Artillery
1st Battalion 135th Artillery
2nd Battalion 135th Artillery
1st Battalion 136th Artillery
2nd Battalion 136th Artillery

1st Battalion 137th Armor

2nd Squadron 137th Armor

737th Ordnance Battalion
112th Engineer Battalion
112th Medical Battalion
137th Signal Battalion
537th Transportation Battalion
37th Quartermaster Company
37th Aviation Company
37th Administration Company
37th Aircraft Maintenance Detachment

38th Infantry Division-National Guard-Cyclone-1960

1st Battle Group 151st Infantry
1st Battle Group 152nd Infantry
2nd Battle Group 152nd Infantry
1st Battle Group 293rd Infantry
2nd Battle Group 293rd Infantry

1st Battalion 139th Artillery
2nd Battalion 139th Artillery
3rd Battalion 139th Artillery
1st Battalion 150th Artillery
2nd Battalion 150th Artillery
1st Battalion 293rd Artillery

1st Battalion 138th Armor

2nd Squadron 138th Armor

738th Ordnance Battalion
113th Engineer Battalion
113th Medical Battalion
138th Signal Battalion
538th Transportation Battalion
38th Quartermaster Company
38th Aviation Company
38th Administration Company
38th Aircraft Maintenance Detachment

39th Infantry Division-National Guard-Delta-1960

1st Battle Group 153rd Infantry
2nd Battle Group 153rd Infantry
1st Battle Group 156th Infantry
2nd Battle Group 156th Infantry
3rd Battle Group 156th Infantry

1st Battalion 141st Artillery
2nd Battalion 141st Artillery
3rd Battalion 141st Artillery
1st Battalion 206th Artillery
2nd Battalion 206th Artillery
3rd Battalion 206th Artillery

1st Battalion 139th Armor

1st Squadron 206th Armor

739th Ordnance Battalion
217th Engineer Battalion
125th Medical Battalion
139th Signal Battalion
539th Transportation Battalion
39th Quartermaster Company
39th Aviation Company
39th Administration Company
539th Aircraft Maintenance Detachment

41st Infantry Division-National Guard-Sunset-1960

1st Battle Group 161st Infantry
2nd Battle Group 161st Infantry
1st Battle Group 162nd Infantry
1st Battle Group 186th Infantry
2nd Battle Group 186th Infantry

1st Battalion 146th Artillery
2nd Battalion 146th Artillery
1st Battalion 218th Artillery
2nd Battalion 218th Artillery
3rd Battalion 218th Artillery
1st Battalion 248th Artillery

1st Battalion 303rd Armor

1st Squadron 82nd Armor

741st Ordnance Battalion
162nd Engineer Battalion
116th Medical Battalion
241st Signal Battalion
241st Transportation Battalion
41st Quartermaster Company
41st Aviation Company
41st Administration Company
41st Aircraft Maintenance Detachment

42nd Infantry Division-National Guard-Rainbow-1960

1st Battle Group 71st Infantry
1st Battle Group 106th Infantry
1st Battle Group 107th Infantry
1st Battle Group 165th Infantry
1st Battle Group 251st Infantry

2nd Battalion 104th Artillery
1st Battalion 105th Artillery
1st Battalion 258th Artillery
2nd Battalion 258th Artillery

3rd Battalion 258th Artillery
4th Battalion 258th Artillery

1st Battalion 142nd Armor

1st Squadron 101st Armor

42nd Ordnance Battalion
102nd Engineer Battalion
102nd Medical Battalion
242nd Signal Battalion
642nd Transportation Battalion
42nd Quartermaster Company
42nd Aviation Company
42nd Administration Company
642nd Aircraft Maintenance Detachment

43rd Infantry Division-National Guard-Red Wing-1960

1st Battle Group 102nd Infantry
2nd Battle Group 102nd Infantry
1st Battle Group 169th Infantry
2nd Battle Group 169th Infantry
1st Battle Group 172nd Infantry

1st Battalion 103rd Artillery
2nd Battalion 103rd Artillery
3rd Battalion 103rd Artillery
4th Battalion 103rd Artillery
1st Battalion 124th Artillery
1st Battalion 242nd Artillery

1st Battalion 172nd Armor

2nd Squadron 172nd Armor

743rd Ordnance Battalion
118th Engineer Battalion
118th Medical Battalion
243rd Signal Battalion
143rd Transportation Battalion

43rd Quartermaster Company
43rd Aviation Company
43rd Administration Company
143rd Aircraft Maintenance Detachment

45th Infantry Division-National Guard-Thunderbirds-1960

1st Battle Group 179th Infantry
2nd Battle Group 179th Infantry
1st Battle Group 180th Infantry
2nd Battle Group 180th Infantry
1st Battle Group 279th Infantry

1st Battalion 158th Artillery
2nd Battalion 158th Artillery
1st Battalion 160th Artillery
2nd Battalion 160th Artillery
1st Battalion 189th Artillery
2nd Battalion 189th Artillery

1st Battalion 245th Armor

2nd Squadron 245th Armor

700th Ordnance Battalion
120th Engineer Battalion
120th Medical Battalion
145th Signal Battalion
245th Transportation Battalion
45th Quartermaster Company
45th Aviation Company
45th Administration Company
245th Aircraft Maintenance Detachment

46th Infantry Division-National Guard-Ironfist-1960

1st Battle Group 125th Infantry
2nd Battle Group 125th Infantry
1st Battle Group 126th Infantry
2nd Battle Group 126th Infantry

1st Battle Group 225th Infantry

1st Battalion 119th Artillery
2nd Battalion 119th Artillery
3rd Battalion 119th Artillery
1st Battalion 182nd Artillery
2nd Battalion 182nd Artillery
3rd Battalion 182nd Artillery

2nd Battalion 246th Armor

1st Squadron 246th Armor

107th Ordnance Battalion
107th Engineer Battalion
107th Medical Battalion
107th Signal Battalion
46th Quartermaster Company
46th Aviation Company
46th Administration Company
146th Aircraft Maintenance Detachment

47th Infantry Division-National Guard-Viking-1960

1st Battle Group 135th Infantry
2nd Battle Group 135th Infantry
1st Battle Group 136th Infantry
2nd Battle Group 136th Infantry
3rd Battle Group 136th Infantry

1st Battalion 125th Artillery
2nd Battalion 125th Artillery
3rd Battalion 125th Artillery
1st Battalion 151st Artillery
2nd Battalion 151st Artillery
3rd Battalion 151st Artillery

1st Battalion 194th Armor

2nd Squadron 194th Armor

747th Ordnance Battalion
682nd Engineer Battalion
204th Medical Battalion
147th Signal Battalion
147th Transportation Battalion
47th Quartermaster Company
47th Aviation Company
47th Administration Company
147th Aircraft Maintenance Detachment

49th Infantry Division-National Guard-Argonaunt-1960

1st Battle Group 159th Infantry
2nd Battle Group 159th Infantry
1st Battle Group 184th Infantry
2nd Battle Group 184th Infantry
1st Battle Group 185th Infantry

1st Battalion 143rd Artillery
2nd Battalion 143rd Artillery
3rd Battalion 143rd Artillery
4th Battalion 143rd Artillery
5th Battalion 143rd Artillery
6th Battalion 143rd Artillery

1st Battalion 149th Armor

2nd squadron 149th Armor

749th Ordnance Battalion
579th Engineer Battalion
126th Medical Battalion
49th Signal Battalion
249th Transportation Battalion
49th Quartermaster Company
49th Aviation Company
49th Administration Company
249th Aircraft Maintenance Detachment

51st Infantry Division-National Guard-Rattlesnake-1960

1st Battle Group 118th Infantry
2nd battle Group 118th Infantry
3rd Battle Group 118th Infantry
1st Battle Group 211th Infantry
2nd Battle Group 211th Infantry

1st Battalion 116th Artillery
3rd Battalion 116th Artillery
1st Battalion 178th Artillery
2nd Battalion 178th Artillery
3rd Battalion 178th Artillery
4th Battalion 178th Artillery

1st Battalion 263rd Armor

2nd Squadron 263rd Armor

751st Ordnance Battalion
132nd Engineer Battalion
201st Medical Battalion
151st Signal Battalion
151st Transportation Battalion
51st Quartermaster Company
51st Aviation Company
51st Administration Company
151st Aircraft Maintenance Detachment

63rd Infantry Division-Army Reserve-Blood & Fire-1960

3rd Battle Group 15th Infantry
3rd Battle Group 21st Infantry
3rd Battle Group 27th Infantry
3rd Battle Group 30th Infantry
3rd Battle Group 31st Infantry

6th Battalion 4th Artillery
5th Battalion 11th Artillery
5th Battalion 19th Artillery
4th Battalion 21st Artillery

5th Battalion 35th Artillery
3rd Battalion 77th Artillery

7th Battalion 40th Armor

5th Squadron 8th Cavalry

763rd Ordnance Battalion
263rd Engineer Battalion
363rd Medical Battalion
163rd Signal Battalion
63rd Transportation Battalion
63rd Quartermaster Company
63rd Aviation Company
63rd Administration Company
63rd Aircraft Maintenance Detachment

70th Division Training-Army Reserve-Trailblazer-1960

70th Regiment-CST
329th Regiment-BCT
330th Regiment-BCT
333rd Regiment-BCT
423rd Regiment-AIT

Headquarters Company
Receiving Company
Support Company
Test Company
Transportation Company
NCO Academy

76th Division Training-Army Reserve-Onaway-1960

76th Regiment-CST
304th Regiment-BCT
385th Regiment-BCT
417th Regiment-BCT
418th Regiment-AIT

Headquarters Company
Receiving Company
Support Company
Test Company
Transportation Company
NCO Academy

77th Infantry Division-Army Reserve-Statue of Liberty-1960

3rd Battle Group 1st Infantry
3rd Battle Group 26th Infantry
1st Battle Group 305th Infantry
1st Battle Group 306th Infantry
1st Battle Group 307th Infantry

7th Battalion 4th Artillery
6th Battalion 5th Artillery
6th Battalion 7th Artillery
5th Battalion 12th Artillery
6th Battalion 31st Artillery
3rd Battalion 73rd Artillery

5th Battalion 68th Armor

3rd Squadron 8th Cavalry

777th Ordnance Battalion
302nd Engineer Battalion
302nd Medical Battalion
77th Signal Battalion
77th Transportation Battalion
77th Quartermaster Company
77th Aviation Company
77th Administration Company
77th Aircraft Maintenance Detachment

78th Division Training-Army Reserve-Lightning-1960

78th Regiment-CST
309th Regiment-BCT
310th Regiment-BCT
311th Regiment-BCT
312th Regiment-AIT

Headquarters Company
Receiving Company
Support Company
Test Company
Transportation Company
NCO Academy

79th Infantry Division-Army Reserve-Cross of Lorraine-1960

3rd Battle Group 12th Infantry
3rd Battle Group 34th Infantry
1st Battle Group 305th Infantry
1st Battle Group 306th Infantry
1st Battle Group 307th Infantry

6th Battalion 1st Artillery
7th Battalion 6th Artillery
4th Battalion 9th Artillery
3rd Battalion 15th Artillery
3rd Battalion 27th Artillery
5th Battalion 37th Artillery

6th Battalion 68th Armor

3rd Squadron 9th Cavalry

779th Ordnance Battalion
304th Engineer Battalion
304th Medical Battalion
179th Signal Battalion
279th Transportation Battalion
79th Quartermaster Company
79th Aviation Company

79th Administration Company
79th Aircraft Maintenance Detachment

80th Division Training-Army Reserve-Blue Ridge-1960

80th Regiment-CST
317th Regiment-BCT
318th Regiment-BCT
319th Regiment-BCT
320th Regiment-AIT

Headquarters Company
Receiving Company
Support Company
Test Company
Transportation Company
NCO Academy

81st Infantry Division-Army Reserve-Wilcat-1960

3rd Battle Group 29th Infantry
4th Battle Group 32nd Infantry
3rd Battle Group 47th Infantry
1st Battle Group 322nd Infantry
1st Battle Group 345th Infantry

3rd Battalion 8th Artillery
4th Battalion 10th Artillery
4th Battalion 12th Artillery
4th Battalion 16th Artillery
5th Battalion 18th Artillery
5th Battalion 22nd Artillery

5th Battalion 68th Armor

3rd Squadron 15th Cavalry

781st Ordnance Battalion
306th Engineer Battalion

306th Medical Battalion
181st Signal Battalion
81st Transportation Battalion
81st Quartermaster Company
81st Aviation Company
81st Administration Company
81st Aircraft Maintenance Detachment

82nd Airborne Division-Active Component-All American-1960

1st Airborne Battle Group 187th Infantry
1st Airborne Battle Group 325th Infantry
2nd Airborne Battle Group 502nd Infantry
1st Airborne Battle Group 503rd Infantry
2nd Airborne Battle Group 504th Infantry

Battery A 319th Artillery
Battery B 319th Artillery
Battery C 319th Artillery
Battery C 320th Artillery
Battery D 320th Artillery
Battery B 377th Artillery

Troop A 17th Cavalry

782nd Ordnance Battalion
307th Engineer Battalion
307th Medical Battalion
82nd Signal Battalion
82nd Transportation Battalion
82nd Quartermaster Company
82nd Aviation Company
82nd Administration Company
82nd Aircraft Maintenance Detachment

83rd Infantry Division-Army Reserve-Thunderbolt-1960

3rd Battle Group 2nd infantry
3rd Battle Group 10th Infantry
3rd Battle Group 11th Infantry

4th Battle Group 19th Infantry
3rd Battle Group 28th Infantry

7th Battalion 1st Artillery
3rd Battalion 9th Artillery
5th Battalion 14th Artillery
5th Battalion 15th Artillery
4th Battalion 27th Artillery
7th Battalion 28th artillery

7th Battalion 68th Armor

4th Squadron 8th Cavalry

783rd Ordnance Battalion
308th Engineer Battalion
308th Medical Battalion
83rd Signal Battalion
83rd Transportation Battalion
83rd Quartermaster Company
83rd Aviation Company
83rd Administration Company
83rd Aircraft Maintenance Detachment

84th Division Training-Army Reserve-Railsplitters-1960

84th Regiment-CST
274th Regiment-BCT
334th Regiment-BCT
339th Regiment-BCT
351st Regiment-AIT

Headquarters Company
Receiving Company
Support Company
Test Company
Transportation Company
NCO Academy

85th Division Training-Army Reserve-Custer-1960

85th Regiment-CST
335th Regiment-BCT
337th Regiment-BCT
338th Regiment-BCT
340th Regiment-AIT

Headquarters Company
Receiving Company
Support Company
Test Company
Transportation Company
NCO Academy
89th Division Training-Army Reserve-Rolling W-1960

89th Regiment-CST
353rd Regiment-BCT
354th Regiment-BCT
355th Regiment-BCT
356th Regiment-AIT

Headquarters Company
Receiving Company
Support Company
Test Company
Transportation Company
NCO Academy

90th Infantry Division-Army Reserve-Tough Ombres-1960

3rd Battle Group 20th Infantry
3rd Battle Group 23rd Infantry
1st Battle Group 357th Infantry
1st Battle Group 358th Infantry
1st Battle Group 359th Infantry

3rd Battalion 12th Artillery
4th Battalion 15th Artillery
5th Battalion 17th Artillery
4th Battalion 19th Artillery

4th Battalion 77th Artillery
3rd Battalion 78th Artillery

5th Battalion 37th Armor

4th Squadron 15th Cavalry

790th Ordnance Battalion
315th Engineer Battalion
315th Medical Battalion
190th Signal Battalion
90th Transportation Battalion
90th Quartermaster Company
90th Aviation Company
90th Administration Company
190th Aircraft Maintenance Detachment

91st Division Training-Army Reserve-Powder River-1960

91st Regiment-AIT
360th Regiment-BCT
361st Regiment-BCT
362nd Regiment-BCT
363rd Regiment-CST

Headquarters Company
Receiving Company
Support Company
Test Company
Transportation Company
NCO Academy

94th Infantry Division-Army Reserve-Neuf Cats-1960

3rd Battle Group 5th Infantry
3rd Battle Group 13th Infantry
3rd Battle Group 16th Infantry
3rd Battle Group 18th Infantry
3rd Battle Group 18th Infantry
3rd Battle Group 35th Infantry

5th Battalion 5th Artillery
7th Battalion 7th Artillery
5th Battalion 10th Artillery
6th Battalion 11th Artillery
3rd Battalion 22nd Artillery
4th Battalion 73rd Artillery

9th Battalion 34th Armor

4th Squadron 5th Cavalry

794th Ordnance Battalion
319th Engineer Battalion
319th Medical Battalion
94th Signal Battalion
94th Transportation Battalion
94th Quartermaster Company
94th Aviation Company
94th Administration Company
94th Aircraft Maintenance Detachment

95th Division Training-Army Reserve-Iron Men of Metz-1960

95th Regiment-CST
291st Regiment-BCT
377th Regiment-BCT
378th Regiment-BCT
379th Regiment-AIT

Headquarters Company
Receiving Company
Support Company
Test Company
Transportation Company
NCO Academy

96th Infantry Division-Army Reserve-Deadeyes-1960

3rd Battle Group 22nd Infantry
3rd Battle Group 38th Infantry
1st Battle Group 59th Infantry
1st Battle Group 381st Infantry
1st Battle Group 383rd Infantry

4th Battalion 2nd Artillery
5th Battalion 9th Artillery
4th Battalion 11th Artillery
5th Battalion 21st Artillery
5th Battalion 34th Artillery
4th Battalion 35th Artillery

8th Battalion 40th Armor

4th Squadron 8th Cavalry

796th Ordnance Battalion
321st Engineer Battalion
321st Medical Battalion
96th Signal Battalion
96th Transportation Battalion
96th Quartermaster Company
96th Aviation Company
96th Administration Company
96th Aircraft Maintenance Detachment

98th Division Training-Army Reserve-Iroquois-1960

98th Regiment-CST
389th Regiment-BCT
390th Regiment-BCT
391st Regiment-BCT
392nd Regiment-AIT

Headquarters Company
Receiving Company
Support Company
Test Company

Transportation Company
NCO Academy

100th Division Training-Army Reserve-Century-1960

100th Regiment-CST
397th Regiment-BCT
398th Regiment-BCT
399th Regiment-BCT
400th Regiment-AIT

Headquarters Company
Receiving Company
Support Company
Test Company
Transportation Company
NCO Academy

101st Airborne Division-Active Component-Screaming Eagles-1960

2nd Battle Group 187th Infantry
1st Battle Group 327th Infantry
1st Battle Group 501st Infantry
1st Battle Group 502nd Infantry
1st Battle Group 506th Infantry

Battery D 319th Artillery
Battery E 319th Artillery
Battery A 321st Artillery
Battery B 321st Artillery
Battery C 321st Artillery

Troop B 17th Cavalry

801st Ordnance Battalion
326th Engineer Battalion
326th Medical Battalion
501st signal Battalion
5th Transportation Battalion
426th Quartermaster Company

101st Aviation Company
101st Administration Company
101st Aircraft Maintenance Detachment

102nd Infantry Division-Army Reserve-Ozark-1960

3rd Battle Group 4th Infantry
4th Battle Group 6th Infantry
3rd Battle Group 7th Infantry
3rd Battle Group 9th Infantry
3rd Battle Group 14th Infantry

4th Battalion 13th Artillery
4th Battalion 14th Artillery
5th Battalion 20th Artillery
3rd Battalion 31st Artillery
4th Battalion 34th Artillery
4th Battalion 78th Artillery

4th Battalion 35th Armor

4th Squadron 4th Cavalry

802nd Ordnance Battalion
327th Engineer Battalion
327th Medical Battalion
202nd Signal Battalion
602nd Transportation Battalion
102nd Quartermaster Company
102nd Aviation Company
102nd Administration Company
102nd Aircraft Maintenance Detachment

103rd Infantry Division-Army Reserve-Catcus-1960

3rd Battle Group 3rd Infantry
3rd Battle Group 17th Infantry
1st Battle Group 409th Infantry
1st Battle Group 410th Infantry
1st Battle Group 411th Infantry

5th Battalion 8th Artillery
6th Battalion 13th Artillery
3rd Battalion 14th Artillery
3rd Battalion 20th Artillery
4th Battalion 31st Artillery
3rd Battalion 34th Artillery

4th Battalion 33rd Armor

5th Squadron 4th Cavalry

803rd Ordnance Battalion
328th Engineer Battalion
328th Medical Battalion
103rd Signal Battalion
103rd Transportation Battalion
103rd Quartermaster Company
103rd Aviation Company
103rd Administration Company
103rd Aircraft Maintenance Detachment

104th Division Training-Army Reserve-Timberwolves-1960

104th Regiment-AIT
413th Regiment-BCT
414th Regiment-BCT
415th Regiment-BCT
416th Regiment-CST

Headquarters Company
Receiving Company
Support Company
Test Company
Transportation Company
NCO Academy

108th Division Training-Army Reserve-Golden Griffon-1960

108th Regiment-CST
321st Regiment-BCT
323rd Regiment-BCT

485th Regiment-BCT
518th Regiment-AIT

Headquarters Company
Receiving Company
Support Company
Test Company
Transportation Company
NCO Academy

1965

1st Infantry Division-Active Component-Big Red One-1965

1st Battalion 2nd Infantry
2nd battalion 2nd Infantry
1st Battalion 16th Infantry
2nd battalion 16th Infantry
1st Battalion 18th Infantry
2nd battalion 18th Infantry
1st Battalion 26th Infantry
1st Battalion 28th Infantry
2nd Battalion 28th Infantry

1st Battalion 5th Artillery
8th Battalion 6th Artillery
1st Battalion 7th Artillery
5th Battalion 32nd Artillery
2nd battalion 33rd Artillery

1st Battalion 63rd Armor
2nd battalion 63rd Armor

1st Squadron 4th cavalry

701st Maintenance Battalion
1st Engineer Battalion
1st Medical Battalion
121st Signal Battalion
1st Aviation Battalion
1st Supply & Transport Battalion
1st Military Police Company
1st Administration Company
337th Army Security Company

2nd Infantry Division-Active Component-Indianhead-1965

1st Battalion 9th Infantry
2nd Battalion 9th Infantry

1st Battalion 23rd Infantry
2nd Battalion 23rd Infantry
3rd Battalion 23rd Infantry
1st Battalion 38th Infantry
2nd Battalion 38th Infantry

1st Battalion 12th Artillery
1st Battalion 15th Artillery
7th Battalion 17th Artillery
6th Battalion 37th Artillery
5th Battalion 38th Artillery

1st Battalion 72nd Armor
2nd Battalion 72nd Armor

4th Squadron 7th Cavalry

702nd Ordnance Battalion
2nd Engineer Battalion
2nd Medical Battalion
122nd Signal Battalion
2nd Aviation Battalion
2nd Supply & Transport Battalion
2nd Military Police Company
2nd Administration Company

3rd Infantry Division-Active Component-Marne-1965

1st Battalion 4th Infantry
1st Battalion 7th Infantry
1st Battalion 15th Infantry
2nd Battalion 15th Infantry
1st Battalion 30th Infantry
2nd Battalion 30th Infantry

1st Battalion 9th Artillery
1st Battalion 10th Artillery
2nd Battalion 39th Artillery
2nd Battalion 41st Artillery
3rd Battalion 76th Artillery

1st Battalion 64th Armor
2nd Battalion 64th Armor
3rd Battalion 64th Armor
4th Battalion 64th Armor

3rd Squadron 7th Cavalry

703rd Maintenance Battalion
10th Engineer Battalion
3rd Medical Battalion
123rd Signal Battalion
3rd Aviation Battalion
3rd Supply & Transport Battalion
3rd Military Police Company
3rd Administration Company

4th Infantry Division-Active Component-Ivy-1965

1st Battalion 8th Infantry
2nd Battalion 8th Infantry
3rd Battalion 8th Infantry
1st Battalion 12th Infantry
2nd Battalion 12th Infantry
3rd Battalion 12th Infantry
1st Battalion 22nd Infantry
2nd Battalion 22nd Infantry

5th Battalion 16th Artillery
1st Battalion 20th Artillery
6th Battalion 29th Artillery
4th Battalion 42nd Artillery
2nd Battalion 77th Artillery

2nd Battalion 34th Armor

1st Squadron 10th Cavalry

704th Maintenance Battalion
4th Engineer Battalion
4th Medical Battalion
124th Signal Battalion

4th Aviation Battalion
4th Supply & Transport Battalion
4th Military Police Company
4th Administration Company
374th Army Security Company

5th Infantry Division-Active Component-Red Devils-1965

1st Battalion 10th Infantry
2nd Battalion 10th Infantry
1st Battalion 11th Infantry
2nd Battalion 11th Infantry
1st Battalion 61st Infantry
2nd Battalion 61st Infantry

5th Battalion 4th Artillery
1st Battalion 19th Artillery
6th Battalion 20th Artillery
6th Battalion 21st Artillery
1st Battalion 29th Artillery

1st Battalion 77th Armor
3rd Battalion 77th Armor

4th Squadron 12th Cavalry

705th Maintenance Battalion
7th Engineer Battalion
5th Medical Battalion
5th Signal Battalion
5th Aviation Battalion
5th Supply Transport Battalion
5th Military Police Company
5th Administration Company

6th Infantry Division-Active Component-Red Star-1967

4th Battalion 1st Infantry
5th Battalion 1st Infantry
6th Battalion 1st Infantry
5th Battalion 3rd Infantry
6th Battalion 3rd Infantry
7th Battalion 3rd Infantry
2nd Battalion 20th Infantry
3rd Battalion 20th Infantry
6th Battalion 20th Infantry

6th Battalion 1st Artillery
5th Battalion 3rd Artillery
6th Battalion 78th Artillery
1st Battalion 80th Artillery

4th Squadron 9th Cavalry

706th Maintenance Battalion
96th Engineer Battalion
6th Medical Battalion
6th Signal Battalion
6th Aviation Battalion
6th Supply & Transport Battalion
6th Military police Company
6th Administration Company

7th Infantry Division-Active Component-Bayonet-1965

1st Battalion 17th Infantry
2nd Battalion 17th Infantry
1st Battalion 31st Infantry
2nd Battalion 31st Infantry
1st Battalion 32nd Infantry
2nd Battalion 32nd Infantry
3rd Battalion 32nd Infantry

2nd Battalion 8th Artillery
1st Battalion 31st Artillery
4th Battalion 76th Artillery

1st Battalion 79th Artillery
1st Battalion 80th Artillery

1st Battalion 73rd Armor

2nd Squadron 10th Cavalry

707th Maintenance Battalion
13th Engineer Battalion
7th Medical Battalion
127th Signal Battalion
7th Aviation Battalion
7th Supply & Transport Battalion
7th Military Police Company
7th Administration Company

8th Infantry Division-Active Component-Pathfinders-1965

1st Battalion 13th Infantry
2nd Battalion 13th Infantry
1st Battalion 39th Infantry
1st Battalion 87th Infantry
2nd Battalion 87th Infantry
1st Battalion 509th Infantry
2nd Battalion 509th Infantry

1st Battalion 2nd Artillery
7th Battalion 16th Artillery
1st Battalion 28th Artillery
5th Battalion 81st Artillery
5th Battalion 83rd Artillery

1st Battalion 68th Armor
2nd Battalion 68th Armor
3rd Battalion 68th Armor

3rd Squadron 8th Cavalry

708th Maintenance Battalion
12th Engineer Battalion
8th Medical Battalion

128th Signal Battalion
8th Aviation Battalion
8th Supply & Transport Battalion
8th Military Police Company
8th Administration Company

9th Infantry Division-Active Component-Old Reliables-1965

2nd Battalion 39th Infantry
3rd Battalion 39th Infantry
4th Battalion 39th Infantry
2nd Battalion 47th Infantry
3rd Battalion 47th Infantry
4th Battalion 47th Infantry
2nd Battalion 60th Infantry
3rd Battalion 60th Infantry
5th Battalion 60th Infantry

2nd Battalion 4th Artillery
1st Battalion 11th Artillery
3rd Battalion 28th Artillery
3rd Battalion 34th Artillery
1st Battalion 84th Artillery

3rd Squadron 9th Cavalry

709th Maintenance Battalion
15th Engineer Battalion
9th Medical Battalion
9th Signal Battalion
9th Aviation Battalion
9th Supply & Transport Battalion
9th Military Police Company
335th Army Security Company

11th Air Assault Division-Active Component-Angels-1965

1st Battalion 187th Infantry
1st Battalion 188th Infantry
1st Battalion 511th Infantry

2nd Battalion 42nd Artillery
6th Battalion 81st Artillery
3rd Battalion 377th Artillery
Battery E 26th Artillery

3rd Squadron 17th Cavalry

711th Maintenance Battalion
127th Engineer Battalion
11th Medical Battalion
511th Signal Battalion
11th Aviation Group
226th Aerial Surveillance & Escort Battalion
227th 228th 229th Assault Helicopter Battalions
11th General Support Aviation Company
408th Service & Supply Company
611th Aircraft Maintenance4 & Support Battalion
11th Aviation Pathfinder Company
11th Administration Company

23rd Infantry Division-Active Component-Americal-1965

2nd Battalion 1st Infantry
3rd Battalion 1st Infantry
4th Battalion 3rd Infantry
1st Battalion 6th Infantry
1st Battalion 20th Infantry
3rd Battalion 21st Infantry
4th Battalion 21st Infantry
1st Battalion 46th Infantry
5th Battalion 46th Infantry
1st Battalion 52nd Infantry

6th Battalion 11th Artillery
1st Battalion 14th Artillery
3rd Battalion 16th Artillery
3rd Battalion 18th Artillery
1st Battalion 82nd Artillery
3rd Battalion 82nd Artillery
Battery G 55th Artillery

Troop E 1st Cavalry
Troop F 8th Cavalry
Troop H 17th Cavalry

723rd Maintenance Battalion
26th Engineer Battalion
23rd Medical Battalion
523rd Signal Battalion
23rd Aviation Battalion
23rd Supply & Transport Battalion
23rd Military Police Company
23rd Administration Company
328th Army Security Company

24th Infantry Division-Active Component-Victory-1965

1st Battalion 19th Infantry
2nd Battalion 19th Infantry
3rd Battalion 19th Infantry
1st Battalion 21st Infantry
2nd Battalion 21st Infantry
1st Battalion 34th Infantry
2nd Battalion 34th Infantry

2nd Battalion 7th Artillery
3rd Battalion 11th Artillery
1st Battalion 13th Artillery
1st Battalion 34th Artillery
1st Battalion 35th Artillery

1st Battalion 70th Armor
2nd Battalion 70th Armor
3rd Battalion 70th Armor

2nd Squadron 9th Cavalry

724th Maintenance Battalion
3rd Engineer Battalion
24th Medical Battalion
24th Signal Battalion
24th Aviation Battalion

24th Supply & Transport Battalion
24th Military Police Company
24th Administration Company

25th Infantry Division-Active Component-Tropic Lightning-1966

1st Battalion 5th Infantry
4th Battalion 9th Infantry
1st Battalion 14th Infantry
2nd Battalion 14th Infantry
4th Battalion 23rd Infantry
1st Battalion 27th Infantry
2nd Battalion 27th Infantry
1st Battalion 35th Infantry
2nd Battalion 35th Infantry

1st Battalion 8th Artillery
2nd Battalion 9th Artillery
7th Battalion 11th Artillery
3rd Battalion 13th Artillery
2nd Battalion 21st Artillery

1st Battalion 69th Armor

3rd Squadron 4th Cavalry

725th Maintenance Battalion
65th Engineer Battalion
25th Medical Battalion
125th Signal Battalion
25th Aviation Battalion
25th Supply & Transport Battalion
25th Military Police Company
25th Administration Company
372nd Army Security Company
1st 2nd 3rd Support Battalions (Provisional)

26th Infantry Division-National Guard-Yankee-1965

1st Battalion 101st Infantry
1st Battalion 104th Infantry
2nd Battalion 104th Infantry
1st Battalion 181st Infantry
1st Battalion 182nd Infantry
1st Battalion 220th Infantry

1st Battalion 101st Artillery
2nd Battalion 101st Artillery
3rd Battalion 101st Artillery
1st Battalion 102nd Artillery
2nd Battalion 102nd Artillery

1st Battalion 110th Armor
2nd Battalion 110th Armor

1st Squadron 26th Cavalry

726th Maintenance Battalion
114th Engineer Battalion
101st Medical Battalion
126th Signal Battalion
26th Aviation Battalion
26th Supply & Transport Battalion
26th Military Police Company
26th Administration Company

28th Infantry Division-National Guard-Keystone-1965

1st Battalion 109th Infantry
2nd Battalion 109th Infantry
1st Battalion 110th Infantry
1st Battalion 111th Infantry
2nd Battalion 111th Infantry
1st Battalion 112th Infantry

1st Battalion 107th Artillery
1st Battalion 108th Artillery
1st Battalion 109th Artillery

1st Battalion 166th Artillery
1st Battalion 229th Artillery

1st Battalion 103rd Armor
2nd Battalion 103rd Armor

1st Squadron 223rd Cavalry

728th Maintenance Battalion
103rd Engineer Battalion
103rd Medical Battalion
28th Signal Battalion
28th Aviation Battalion
28th Supply & Transport Battalion
28th Military Police Company
28th Administration Company

29th Infantry Division-National Guard-Blue & Gray-1965

1st Battalion 115th Infantry
2nd Battalion 115th Infantry
1st Battalion 116th Infantry
2nd Battalion 116th Infantry
1st Battalion 175th Infantry
2nd Battalion 175th Infantry

1st Battalion 110th Artillery
2nd Battalion 110th Artillery
1st Battalion 111th Artillery
1st Battalion 246th Artillery
2nd Battalion 246th Artillery

1st Battalion 115th Armor
1st Battalion 116th Armor

1st Squadron 183rd Cavalry

729th Maintenance Battalion
121st Engineer Battalion
104th Medical Battalion
129th Signal Battalion

29th Aviation ?Battalion
229th Supply & Transport Battalion
29th Military Police Company
29th Administration Company

30th Infantry Division-National Guard-Old Hickory-1965

4th Battalion 119th Infantry
5th Battalion 119th Infantry
6th Battalion 119th Infantry
1st Battalion 120th Infantry
2nd Battalion 120th Infantry
3rd Battalion 120th Infantry

1st Battalion 113th Artillery
2nd Battalion 113th Artillery
3rd Battalion 113th Artillery
4th Battalion 113th Artillery
5th Battalion 113th Artillery

1st Battalion 252nd Armor
2nd Battalion 252nd Armor

1st Squadron 196th Cavalry

730th Maintenance Battalion
105th Engineer Battalion
105th Medical Battalion
130th Signal Battalion
30th Aviation Battalion
230th Supply & Transport Battalion
30th Military Police Company
30th Administration Company

31st Infantry Division-National Guard-Dixie-1965

1st Battalion 155th Infantry
2nd Battalion 155th Infantry
3rd Battalion 155th Infantry
1st Battalion 167th Infantry

1st Battalion 200th Infantry
2nd Battalion 200th Infantry

1st Battalion 114th Artillery
2nd Battalion 114th Artillery
3rd Battalion 114th Artillery
1st Battalion 117th Artillery
2nd Battalion 117th Artillery

1st Battalion 152nd Armor
1st Battalion 198th Armor

1st Squadron 98th Cavalry

731st Maintenance Battalion
106th Engineer Battalion
106th Medical Battalion
131st Signal Battalion
31st Aviation Battalion
31st Supply & Transport Battalion
31st Military Police Company
31st Administration Company

32nd Infantry Division-National Guard-Red Arrow-1965

1st Battalion 127th Infantry
2nd Battalion 127th Infantry
3rd Battalion 127th Infantry
1st Battalion 128th Infantry
2nd Battalion 128th Infantry
3rd Battalion 128th Infantry

1st Battalion 120th Artillery
2nd Battalion 120th Artillery
1st Battalion 121st Artillery
1st Battalion 126th Artillery
2nd Battalion 126th Artillery

1st Battalion 632nd Armor
2nd Battalion 632nd Armor

1st Squadron 105th Cavalry

732nd Maintenance Battalion
724th Engineer Battalion
135th Medical Battalion
132nd signal Battalion
32nd Aviation Battalion
32nd Supply & Transport Battalion
32nd Military Police Company
32nd Administration Company

33rd Infantry Division-National Guard-Prairie-1965

1st Battalion 129th Infantry
2nd Battalion 129th Infantry
1st Battalion 130th Infantry
2nd Battalion 130th Infantry
3rd Battalion 130th Infantry
1st Battalion 131st Infantry

1st Battalion 122nd Artillery
2nd Battalion 122nd Artillery
3rd Battalion 122nd Artillery
1st Battalion 123rd Artillery
2nd Battalion 123rd Artillery

1st Battalion 126th Armor
2nd Battalion 126th Armor

1st Squadron 106th Cavalry

733rd Maintenance Battalion
108th Engineer Battalion
108th Medical Battalion
133rd Signal Battalion
33rd Aviation Battalion
33rd Supply & Transport Battalion
33rd Military Police Company
33rd Administration Company

36th Infantry Division-National Guard-Texas-1965

1st Battalion 141st Infantry
2nd Battalion 141st Infantry
1st Battalion 142nd Infantry
2nd Battalion 142nd Infantry
2nd Battalion 143rd Infantry
3rd Battalion 143rd Infantry

1st Battalion 131st Artillery
2nd Battalion 133rd Artillery
3rd Battalion 133rd Artillery
4th Battalion 133rd Artillery
5th Battalion 133rd Artillery

6th Battalion 112th Armor
7th Battalion 112th Armor

1st Squadron 124th Cavalry

736th Maintenance Battalion
111th Engineer Battalion
111th Medical Battalion
136th Signal Battalion
36th Aviation Battalion
111th Supply & Transport Battalion
36th Military Police Company
36th Administration Company

37th Infantry Division-National Guard-Buckeyes-1965

1st Battalion 145th Infantry
3rd Battalion 145th Infantry
1st Battalion 147th Infantry
1st Battalion 148th Infantry
2nd Battalion 148th Infantry
1st Battalion 166th Infantry

1st Battalion 134th Artillery
2nd Battalion 134th Artillery
1st Battalion 135th Artillery

1st Battalion 136th Artillery
2nd Battalion 136th Artillery

1st Battalion 137th Armor
2nd Battalion 137th Armor

1st Squadron 237th Cavalry

737th Maintenance Battalion
112th Engineer Battalion
112th Medical Battalion
137th Signal Battalion
37th Aviation Battalion
37th Supply & Transport Battalion
37th Military Police Company
37th Administration Company

38th Infantry Division-National Guard-Cyclone-1965

1st Battalion 151st Infantry
2nd battalion 151st Infantry
1st Battalion 152nd Infantry
2nd Battalion 152nd Infantry
1st Battalion 293rd Infantry
2nd Battalion 293rd Infantry

1st Battalion 139th Artillery
2nd Battalion 139th Artillery
3rd Battalion 139th Artillery
1st Battalion 150th Artillery
2nd Battalion 150th Artillery

1st Battalion 138th Armor
2nd Battalion 138th Armor

1st Squadron 238th Cavalry

738th Maintenance Battalion
113th Engineer Battalion
113th Medical Battalion
138th Signal Battalion

38th Aviation Battalion
38th Supply & Transport Battalion
38th Military Police Company
38th Administration Company

39th Infantry Division-National Guard-Delta-1965

1st Battalion 153rd Infantry
2nd Battalion 153rd Infantry
1st Battalion 156th Infantry
2nd battalion 156th Infantry
3rd Battalion 156th Infantry
4th Battalion 156th Infantry

1st Battalion 141st Artillery
2nd Battalion 141st Artillery
3rd Battalion 142nd Artillery
1st Battalion 206th Artillery
2nd Battalion 206th Artillery

1st Battalion 206th Armor
2nd Battalion 206th Armor

1st Squadron 139th Cavalry

739th Maintenance Battalion
217th Engineer Battalion
125th Medical Battalion
139th Signal Battalion
39th Aviation Battalion
39th Supply & Transport Battalion
39th Military Police Company
39th Administration Company

41st Infantry Division-National Guard-Sunset-1965

1st Battalion 161st Infantry
2nd Battalion 161st Infantry
1st Battalion 162nd Infantry
2nd Battalion 162nd Infantry

1st Battalion 186th Infantry
2nd Battalion 186th Infantry

1st Battalion 146th Artillery
2nd Battalion 146th Artillery
1st Battalion 218th artillery
2nd Battalion 218th Artillery
3rd Battalion 218th Artillery

1st Battalion 303rd Armor
2nd Battalion 303rd Armor

1st Squadron 82nd Cavalry

741st Maintenance Battalion
162nd Engineer Battalion
116th Medical Battalion
241st Signal Battalion
41st Aviation Battalion
41st Supply & Transport Battalion
41st Military Police Company
41st Administration Company

42nd Infantry Division-National Guard-Rainbow-1965

1st Battalion 69th Infantry
2nd Battalion 69th Infantry
1st Battalion 71st Infantry
1st Battalion 106th Infantry
1st Battalion 107th Infantry
2nd Battalion 107th Infantry

2nd Battalion 104th Artillery
1st Battalion 105th Artillery
1st Battalion 258th Artillery
2nd Battalion 258th Artillery
4th Battalion 258th Artillery

1st Battalion 142nd Armor
2nd Battalion 142nd Armor

1st Squadron 101st Cavalry

42nd Maintenance Battalion
102nd Engineer Battalion
102nd Medical Battalion
242nd Signal Battalion
42nd Aviation Battalion
42nd Supply & Transport Battalion
42nd Military Police Company
42nd Administration Company

45th Infantry Division-National Guard-Thunderbirds-1965

1st Battalion 179th Infantry
2nd Battalion 179th Infantry
1st Battalion 180th Infantry
2nd Battalion 180th Infantry
1st Battalion 279th Infantry
2nd Battalion 279th Infantry

1st Battalion 158th Artillery
1st Battalion 160th Artillery
1st Battalion 171st Artillery
1st Battalion 189th Artillery
2nd Battalion 189th Artillery

1st Battalion 245th Armor
2nd Battalion 245th Armor

1st Squadron 145th Cavalry

700th Maintenance Battalion
120th Engineer Battalion
120th Medical Battalion
145th Signal Battalion
45th Aviation Battalion
120th Supply & Transport Battalion
45th Military Police Company
45th Administration Company

46th Infantry Division-National Guard-Ironfist-1965

1st Battalion 125th Infantry
2nd Battalion 125th Infantry
1st Battalion 126th Infantry
2nd Battalion 126th Infantry
3rd Battalion 126th Infantry
1st Battalion 225th Infantry

1st Battalion 119th Artillery
2nd Battalion 119th Artillery
1st Battalion 182nd Artillery
2nd Battalion 182nd Artillery
3rd Battalion 182nd Artillery

2nd Battalion 246th Armor
3rd Battalion 246th Armor

1st Squadron 146th Cavalry

107th Maintenance Battalion
107th Engineer Battalion
107th Medical Battalion
107th Signal Battalion
46th Aviation Battalion
46th Supply & Transport Battalion
46th Military Police Company
46th Administration Company

47th Infantry Division-National Guard-Viking-1965

1st Battalion 135th Infantry
2nd Battalion 135th Infantry
3rd Battalion 135th Infantry
4th Battalion 135th Infantry
1st Battalion 136th Infantry
2nd Battalion 136th Infantry

2nd Battalion 125th Artillery
3rd Battalion 125th Artillery

1st Battalion 151st Artillery
3rd Battalion 151st Artillery
1st Battalion 175th Artillery

1st Battalion 194th Armor
2nd Battalion 194th Armor

1st Battalion 94th Cavalry

747th Maintenance Battalion
682nd Engineer Battalion
204th Medical Battalion
147th Signal Battalion
47th Aviation Battalion
47th Supply & Transport Battalion
47th Military Police Company
47th Administration Company

49th Infantry Division-National Guard-Argonaunt-1965

1st Battalion 159th Infantry
2nd Battalion 159th Infantry
1st Battalion 184th Infantry
2nd Battalion 184th Infantry
1st Battalion 185th Infantry
2nd Battalion 185th Infantry

1st Battalion 143rd Artillery
2nd Battalion 143rd Artillery
3rd Battalion 143rd Artillery
4th Battalion 143rd Artillery
5th Battalion 143rd Artillery

2nd Battalion 249th Armor
3rd Battalion 249th Armor

1st Squadron 170th Cavalry

749th Maintenance Battalion
579th Engineer Battalion
126th Medical Battalion

49th Signal Battalion
49th Aviation Battalion
249th Supply & Transport Battalion
49th Military Police Company
49th Administration Company

63rd Infantry Division-Army Reserve-Blood & Fire-1965

3rd Battalion 15th Infantry
4th Battalion 15th Infantry
3rd Battalion 27th Infantry
4th Battalion 27th Infantry
3rd Battalion 30th Infantry
3rd Battalion 31st Infantry

6th Battalion 4th Artillery
5th Battalion 11th Artillery
5th Battalion 19th Artillery
4th Battalion 21st Artillery
3rd Battalion 77th Artillery

5th Battalion 40th Armor
7th Battalion 40th Armor

5th Squadron 8th Cavalry

763rd Maintenance Battalion
263rd Engineer Battalion
363rd Medical Battalion
163rd Signal Battalion
63rd Aviation Battalion
63rd Supply & Transport Battalion
63rd Military Police Company
63rd Administration Company

70th Division Training-Army Reserve-Trailblazer-1965

70th Regiment-CST
329th Regiment-BCT
330th Regiment-BCT

333rd Regiment-BCT
423rd Regiment-AIT

Headquarters Company
Receiving Company
Support Company
Test Company
Transportation Company
NCO Academy

76th Division Training-Army Reserve-Onaway-1965

76th Regiment-CST
304th Regiment-BCT
385th Regiment-BCT
417th Regiment-BCT
418th Regiment-AIT

Headquarters Company
Receiving Company
Support Company
Test Company
Transportation Company
NCO Academy

77th Infantry Division-Army Reserve-Statue of Liberty-1965

1st Battalion 305th Infantry
2nd Battalion 305th Infantry
1st Battalion 306th Infantry
2nd Battalion 306th Infantry
1st Battalion 307th Infantry
2nd Battalion 307th Infantry

7th Battalion 4th Artillery
6th Battalion 5th Artillery
6th Battalion 7th Artillery
5th Battalion 12th Artillery
6th Battalion 31st Artillery

6th Battalion 66th Armor
7th Battalion 66th Armor

3rd Squadron 10th Cavalry

777th Maintenance Battalion
302nd Engineer Battalion
302nd Medical Battalion
77th Signal Battalion
77th Aviation Battalion
77th Supply & Transport Battalion
77th Military Police Company
77th Administration Company

78th Division Training-Army Reserve-Lightning-1965

78th Regiment-CST
309th Regiment-BCT
310th Regiment-BCT
311th Regiment-BCT
312th Regiment-AIT

Headquarters Company
Receiving Company
Support Company
Test Company
Transportation Company
NCO Academy

80th Division Training-Army Reserve-Blue Ridge-1965

80th Regiment-CST
317th Regiment-BCT
318th Regiment-BCT
319th Regiment-BCT
320th Regiment-AIT

Headquarters Company
Receiving Company
Test Company
Transportation Company
NCO Academy

81st Infantry Division-Army Reserve-Wildcat-1965

3rd Battalion 29th Infantry
4th Battalion 29th Infantry
1st Battalion 322nd Infantry
2nd Battalion 322nd Infantry
1st Battalion 345th Infantry
2nd Battalion 345th Infantry

3rd Battalion 8th Artillery
4th Battalion 10th Artillery
4th Battalion 12th Artillery
5th Battalion 18th Artillery
4th Battalion 22nd Artillery

5th Battalion 69th Armor
6th Battalion 69th Armor

3rd Squadron 5th Cavalry

781st Maintenance Battalion
306th Engineer Battalion
306th Medical Battalion
181st Signal Battalion
81st Aviation Battalion
81st Supply & Transport Battalion
81st Military Police Company
81st Administration Company

82nd Airborne Division-Active Component-All American-1965

1st Battalion 325th Infantry
2nd Battalion 325th Infantry
3rd Battalion 325th Infantry
1st Battalion 504th Infantry
2nd Battalion 504th Infantry
3rd Battalion 504th Infantry
1st Battalion 505th Infantry
2nd Battalion 505th Infantry
3rd Battalion 505th Infantry

1st Battalion 319th Artillery
1st Battalion 320th Artillery
2nd Battalion 321st Artillery
Battery B 377th Artillery

1st Battalion 16th Armor

1st Squadron 17th Cavalry

782nd Maintenance Battalion
307th Engineer Battalion
307th Medical Battalion
82nd Signal Battalion
82nd Aviation Battalion
407th Supply & Transport Battalion
82nd Military Police Company
82nd Administration Company

83rd Infantry Division-Army Reserve-Thunderbolt-1965

3rd Battalion 2nd Infantry
4th Battalion 2nd Infantry
3rd Battalion 10th Infantry
3rd Battalion 11th Infantry
4th Battalion 11th Infantry
3rd Battalion 28th Infantry

7th Battalion 1st Artillery
3rd Battalion 9th Artillery
5th Battalion 14th Artillery
5th Battalion 15th Artillery
7th Battalion 28th Artillery

7th Battalion 68th Armor
8th Battalion 68th Armor

4th Squadron 8th Cavalry

783rd Maintenance Battalion
308th Engineer Battalion
308th Medical Battalion

83rd Signal Battalion
83rd Aviation Battalion
83rd Supply & Transport Battalion
83rd Military Police Company
83rd Administration Company

84th Division Training-Army Reserve-Railsplitters-1965

84th Regiment-CST
274th Regiment-BCT
334th Regiment-BCT
339th Regiment-BCT
351st Regiment-AIT

Headquarters Company
Receiving Company
Support Company
Test Company
Transportation Company
NCO Academy
85th Division Training-Army Reserve-Custer-1965

85th Regiment-CST
335th Regiment-BCT
337th Regiment-BCT
338th Regiment-BCT
340th Regiment-AIT

Headquarters Company
Receiving Company
Support Company
Test Company
Transportation Company
NCO Academy

89th Division Training-Army Reserve-Rolling W-1965

89th Regiment-CST
353rd Regiment-BCT
354th Regiment-BCT

355th Regiment-BCT
356th Regiment-AIT

Headquarters Company
Receiving Company
Support Company
Test Company
Transportation Company
NCO Academy

90th Infantry Division-Army Reserve-Tough Ombres-1965

1st Battalion 357th Infantry
2nd Battalion 357th Infantry
1st Battalion 358th Infantry
2nd Battalion 358th Infantry
1st Battalion 359th Infantry
2nd Battalion 359th Infantry

3rd Battalion 12th Artillery
4th Battalion 15th Artillery
5th Battalion 17th Artillery
4th Battalion 19th Artillery
3rd Battalion 78th Artillery

3rd Battalion 15th Armor
4th Battalion 15th Armor

5th Squadron 12th Cavalry

790th Maintenance Battalion
315th Engineer Battalion
315th Medical Battalion
190th Signal Battalion
90th Aviation Battalion
90th Supply & Transport Battalion
90th Military Police Company
90th Administration Company

91st Division Training-Army Reserve-Powder River-1965

91st Regiment-AIT
360th Regiment-BCT
361st Regiment-BCT
362nd Regiment-BCT
363rd Regiment-CST

Headquarters Company
Receiving Company
Support Company
Test Company
Transportation Company
NCO Academy

95th Division Training-Army Reserve-Iron Men of Metz-1965

95th Regiment-CST
291st Regiment-BCT
377th Regiment-BCT
378th Regiment-BCT
379th Regiment-AIT

Headquarters Company
Receiving Company
Support Company
Test Company
Transportation Company
NCO Academy

98th Division Training-Army Reserve-Iroquois-1965

98th Regiment-CST
389th Regiment-BCT
390th Regiment-BCT
391st Regiment-BCT
392nd Regiment-AIT

Headquarters Company
Receiving Company

Support Company
Test Company
Transportation Company
NCO Academy

100th Division Training-Army Reserve-Century-1965

100th Regiment-CST
397th Regiment-BCT
398th Regiment-BCT
399th Regiment-BCT
400th Regiment-AIT

Headquarters Company
Receiving Company
Support Company
Test Company
Transportation Company
NCO Academy

101st Airborne Division-Active Component-Screaming Eagles-1965

3rd Battalion 187th Infantry
1st Battalion 327th Infantry
2nd Battalion 327th Infantry
1st Battalion 501st Infantry
2nd Battalion 501st Infantry
1st Battalion 502nd Infantry
2nd Battalion 502nd Infantry
1st Battalion 506th Infantry
2nd Battalion 506th Infantry

2nd Battalion 319th Artillery
2nd Battalion 320th Artillery
1st Battalion 321st Artillery

2nd Battalion 16th Armor

2nd Squadron 17th Cavalry

801st Maintenance Battalion
326th Engineer Battalion
326th Medical Battalion
101st Aviation Battalion
426th Supply & Transport Battalion
101st Military Police Company
101st Administration Company

102nd Infantry Division-Army Reserve-Ozark-1965

3rd Battalion 4th Infantry
4th Battalion 6th Infantry
6th Battalion 6th Infantry
3rd Battalion 9th Infantry
5th Battalion 9th Infantry
3rd Battalion 14th Infantry

4th battalion 13th Artillery
5th Battalion 20th Artillery
3rd Battalion 31st Artillery
4th Battalion 34th Artillery
4th Battalion 78th Artillery

6th Battalion 35th Armor
7th Battalion 35th Armor

4th Squadron 4th Cavalry

802nd Maintenance Battalion
327th Engineer Battalion
327th Medical Battalion
202nd Signal Battalion
102nd Aviation Battalion
102nd Supply & Transport Battalion
102nd Military Police Company
102nd Administration Company

104th Division Training-Army Reserve-Timberwolves-1965

104th Regiment-AIT
413th Regiment-BCT
414th Regiment-BCT
415th Regiment-CST
416th Regiment-BCT

Headquarters Company
Receiving Company
Support Company
Test Company
Transportation Company
NCO Academy

108th Division Training-Army Reserve-Golden Griffon-1965

108th Regiment-CST
321st Regiment-BCT
323rd Regiment-BCT
485th Regiment-AIT
518th Regiment-BCT

Headquarters Company
Receiving Company
Support Company
Test Company
Transportation Company
NCO Academy

2004

1st Infantry Division-Active Component-Big Red One-2004

2nd Battalion 2nd Infantry
1st Battalion 16th Infantry
1st Battalion 18th Infantry
1st Battalion 26th Infantry

1st Battalion 5th Field Artillery
1st Battalion 6th Field Artillery
1st Battalion 7th Field Artillery
1st Battalion 33rd Field Artillery

4th Battalion 3rd Air Defense Artillery

1st Battalion 34th Armor
2nd Battalion 34th Armor
1st Battalion 63rd Armor
2nd Battalion 63rd Armor
1st Battalion 77th Armor

1st Squadron 4th Cavalry
Troops D,E,F 4th Cavalry

1st Battalion 1st Aviation
2nd Battalion 1st Aviation
Company B 3rd Battalion 58th Aviation

701st 101st 201st 299th Support Battalions
601st Aviation Support Battalion
1st 9th 82nd Engineer Battalions
121st Signal Battalion
1st Military Police Company
1st Material Management Center
1st Rear Operations Center
101st Military Intelligence Battalion
1st Chemical Company

2nd Infantry Division-Active Component-Indianhead-2004

2nd Battalion 3rd Infantry-Stryker
1st Battalion 9th Infantry
2nd Battalion 9th Infantry
5th Battalion 20th Infantry-Stryker
1st Battalion 23rd Infantry-Stryker
1st Battalion 503rd Infantry
1st Battalion 506th Infantry
Company D 52nd Infantry-Stryker

1st Battalion 15th Field Artillery
2nd Battalion 17th Field Artillery
1st Battalion 37th Field Artillery-Stryker
6th Battalion 37th Field Artillery
1st Battalion 38th Field Artillery
5th Battalion 5th Air Defense Artillery

1st Battalion 72nd Armor
2nd Battalion 72nd Armor

4th Squadron 7th Cavalry
1st Squadron 14th Cavalry-Stryker

1st Battalion 2nd Aviation
2nd Battalion 2nd Aviation
Company B 4th Battalion 58th Aviation

702nd, 2nd, 302nd Support Battalions
296th Support Battalion-Stryker
602nd Aviation Support Battalion

2nd, 44th Engineer Battalions
18th Engineer Company-Stryker
122nd Signal Battalion
334th Signal Company-Stryker
2nd Military Police Company
2nd Material Management Center
2nd Rear Operations Center
2nd Military Intelligence Battalion
209th Military Intelligence Company-Stryker
4th Chemical Company

3rd Infantry Division-Active Component-Marne-2004

1st Brigade Unit of Action
2nd Battalion 7th Infantry
3rd Battalion 64th Armor
5th Squadron 7th Infantry
1st Battalion 41st Field Artillery
3rd Forward Support Battalion
1st Brigade Troop Battalion

2nd Brigade Unit of Action
3rd Battalion-15th Infantry
1st Battalion-64th Armor
3rd Squadron 7th Cavalry
1st Battalion 9th Field Artillery
26th Forward Support Battalion
2nd Brigade Troop Battalion

3rd Brigade Unit of Action
1st Battalion 15th Infantry
1st Battalion 30th Infantry
2nd Battalion 69th Armor
1st Battalion 10th Field Artillery
203rd Forward Support Battalion
3rd Brigade Troop Battalion

4th Brigade Unit of Action
3rd Battalion 7th Infantry
4th Battalion 64th Armor
6th Squadron 8th Cavalry
1st Battalion 76th Field Artillery
703rd Forward Support Battalion
4th Brigade Troop Battalion

Aviation Brigade
1st Battalion 3rd Aviation
2nd Battalion 3rd Aviation
3rd Battalion 3rd Aviation
4th Battalion 4th Aviation
603rd Aviation Support Battalion

Division Fires Brigade
1st Battalion 39th Field Artillery

Division Support Brigade
87th Corps Support Battalion
3rd Soldier Support Battalion
92nd Engineer Battalion
559th Quartermaster Battalion
260th Quartermaster Battalion
92nd Chemical Company

Special Troop Battalion

4th Infantry Division-Active Component-Ivy-2004

1st Battalion 8th Infantry
2nd Battalion 8th Infantry
1st Battalion 12th Infantry
1st Battalion 22nd Infantry

3rd Battalion 16th Field Artillery
2nd Battalion 20th Field Artillery
3rd Battalion 29th Field Artillery
4th Battalion 42nd Field Artillery

1st Battalion 44th Air Defense Artillery

1st Battalion 66th Armor
3rd Battalion 66th Armor
1st Battalion 67th Armor
3rd Battalion 67th Armor
1st Battalion 68th Armor

1st Squadron 10th Cavalry
Troop B 9th Cavalry
Troops G, H 10th Cavalry

1st Battalion 4th Aviation
2nd Battalion 4th Aviation
Company K 185th Aviation

704th 4th 64th 204th Support Battalions
404th Aviation Support Battalion
4th 299th 588th Engineer Battalions
124th Signal Battalion
4th Military Police Company
4th Material Management Center
4th Rear Operations Center
104th military Intelligence Battalion
31st Chemical Company

7th Infantry Division-Active Component-N.Guard-Bayonet-2004

1st Battalion 153rd Infantry
2nd Battalion 153rd Infantry
3rd Battalion 153rd Infantry
1st Battalion 162nd Infantry
2nd Battalion 162nd Infantry
1st Battalion 179th Infantry
1st Battalion 180th Infantry
1st Battalion 186th Infantry
1st Battalion 279th Infantry

1st Battalion 160th Field Artillery
1st Battalion 206th Field Artillery
2nd Battalion 218th Field Artillery

Battery E 188th Air Defense Artillery
Battery E 202nd Air Defense Artillery
Battery F 202nd Air Defense Artillery

Troop E 82nd Cavalry
Troop E 145th Cavalry
Troop E 151st Cavalry

39th 141st 700th Support Battalions
162nd 239th 245th Engineer Battalions
39th 241st 245th Military Intelligence Companies
10th Infantry Division-Active Component-Mountaineers-2004

1st Brigade Unit of Action

2nd Battalion 22nd Infantry
1st Battalion 87th Infantry
1st Squadron 71st Cavalry
3rd Battalion 6th Field Artillery
10th Forward Support Battalion
1st Brigade Troop Battalion

2nd Brigade Unit of Action
2nd Battalion 14th Infantry
4th Battalion 31st Infantry
2nd Squadron 71st Cavalry
2nd Battalion 15th Field Artillery
210th Forward Support Battalion
2nd Brigade Troop Battalion

3rd Brigade Unit of Action
1st Battalion 32nd Infantry
2nd Battalion 87th Infantry
3rd Squadron 71st Cavalry
4th Battalion 25th Field Artillery
710th Forward Support Battalion
3rd Brigade Troop Battalion

4th Brigade Unit of Action
2nd Battalion 4th Infantry
2nd Battalion 30th Infantry
3rd Squadron 89th Cavalry
5th Battalion 25th Field Artillery
94th Forward Support Battalion
4th Brigade Troop Battalion

Aviation Brigade
1st Battalion 10th Aviation
2nd Battalion 10th Aviation
3rd Battalion 10th Aviation
3rd Squadron 17th Cavalry
277th Aviation Support Battalion

Division Support Brigade
548th Corps Support Battalion
10th Soldier Support Battalion
Special Troop Battalion

24th Infantry Division-Active Component-N.Guard-2004

1st Battalion 118th Infantry
4th Battalion 118th Infantry
1st Battalion 120th Infantry
1st Battalion 121st Infantry
2nd Battalion 121st Infantry

1st Battalion 113th Field Artillery
1st Battalion 118th Field Artillery
1st Battalion 178th Field Artillery

Battery E 179th Air Defense Artillery
Battery G 202nd Air Defense Artillery
Battery E 263rd Air Defense Artillery

1st Battalion 108th Armor
1st Battalion 150th Armor
1st Battalion 252nd Armor
1st Battalion 263rd Armor

Troop E 108th Cavalry
Troop E 196th Cavalry
Troop E 202nd Cavalry

148th 163rd 230th Support Battalions
105th 178th 648th Engineer Battalions
218th 230th 218th Military Intelligence Companies

25th Infantry Division-Active Component-Tropic Lightning-2004

1st Battalion 5th Infantry-Stryker
2nd Battalion 5th Infantry
1st Battalion 14th Infantry
1st Battalion 21st Infantry
3rd Battalion 21st Infantry-Stryker
1st Battalion 24th Infantry-Stryker
1st Battalion 27th Infantry
2nd Battalion 27th Infantry
2nd Battalion 35th Infantry

3rd Battalion 7th Field Artillery
2nd Battalion 8th Field Artillery-Stryker
2nd Battalion 11th Field Artillery
Battery F 7th Field Artillery
25th Field Artillery Detachment

1st Battalion 62nd Air Defense Artillery

3rd Squadron 4th Cavalry
2nd Squadron 14th Cavalry-Styker

1st Battalion 25th Aviation
2nd Battalion 25th Aviation
Company C 25th Aviation
Company G 1st Battalion 58th Aviation

725th 225th 325th Support Battalions
25th Support Battalion-Stryker
65th Engineer Battalion
73rd Signal Company-Stryker
125th Signal Battalion
176th Signal Company-Stryker
25th Military Police Company
125th Military Intelligence Battalion
184th Military Intelligence Company-Stryker

28th Infantry Division-National Guard-Keystone-2004

1st Battalion 109th Infantry
1st Battalion 110th Infantry
1st Battalion 111th Infantry-Stryker
1st Battalion 112th Infantry-Stryker
2nd Battalion 112th Infantry-Stryker
Company D 112th Infantry-Stryker
104th Infantry Detachment

1st Battalion 107th Field Artillery
1st Battalion 108th Field Artillery
1st Battalion 109th Field Artillery
1st Battalion 229th Field Artillery-Stryker
Battery F 109th Field Artillery

1st Battalion 213th Air Defense Artillery

1st Battalion 103rd Armor
2nd Battalion 103rd Armor
3rd Battalion 103rd Armor
1st Battalion 107th Cavalry

1st Squadron 104th Cavalry
2nd Squadron 104th Cavalry-Stryker
Troops I-K 104th Cavalry

1st Battalion 104th Aviation
2nd Battalion 104th Aviation
Company H 104th Aviation

728th 128th 228th Support Battalions
328th Support Battalion-Stryker
756th Support Company-Stryker
628th Aviation Support Battalion
103rd 876th Engineer Battalions
856th Engineer Company-Stryker
1002nd 1303rd Engineer Detachments
28th Signal Battalion
656th Signal Company-Stryker
28th Military Police Company
28th Material Management Center
28th Rear Operations Center
628th Military Intelligence Battalion
556th Military Intelligence Company-Stryker
128th Chemical Company

29th Infantry Division-National Guard-Blue & Gray-2004

1st Battalion 102nd Infantry
1st Battalion 104th Infantry
1st Battalion 115th Infantry
1st Battalion 116th Infantry
2nd Battalion 116th Infantry
3rd Battalion 116th Infantry
1st Battalion 175th Infantry

1st Battalion 181st Infantry
1st Battalion 182nd Infantry
Companies D-E-F 115th Infantry-LAT
129th Infantry Detachment

1st Battalion 101st Field Artillery
2nd Battalion 110th Field Artillery
1st Battalion 246th Field Artillery
Battery E 111th Field Artillery
129th Field Artillery Detachment

3rd Battalion 111th Air Defense Artillery

3rd Battalion 126th Aviation
1st Battalion 130th Aviation
Company F 224th Aviation

1st Squadron 158th Cavalry

729th 143rd 229th 429th Support Battalion
229th Engineer Battalion
1006th Engineer Detachment
129th Signal Battalion
29th Military Police Company
629th Military Intelligence Battalion

34th Infantry Division-National Guard-Red Bull-2004

1st Battalion 133rd Infantry
2nd Battalion 135th Infantry
1st Battalion 136th Infantry
1st Battalion 168th Infantry
194th Infantry Detachment

1st Battalion 125th Field Artillery
1st Battalion 194th Field Artillery
Battery E 151st Field Artillery
Battery F 151st Field Artillery

1st Battalion 216th Air Defense Artillery

1st Battalion 194th Armor
2nd Battalion 194th Armor

1st Squadron 113th Cavalry
Troop G 113th Cavalry

2nd Battalion 147th Aviation
1st Battalion 135th Aviation
Company G 147th Aviation

434th 134th 334th Support Battalions
834th Aviation Support Battalion
434th 534th Support Detachments
682nd Engineer Battalion
834th Engineer Company
1008th 1309th Engineer Detachments
134th Signal Battalion
34th Military Police Company
34th Material Management Center
34th Rear Operations Center
634th Military Intelligence Battalion
434th Chemical Company

35th Infantry Division-National Guard-Santa Fe-2004

2nd Battalion 130th Infantry
1st Battalion 131st Infantry
1st Battalion 167th Infantry
1st Battalion 178th Infantry
134th Infantry Detachment

2nd Battalion 122nd Field Artillery
2nd Battalion 138th Field Artillery
1st Battalion 161st Field Artillery
Battery E 161st Field Artillery
Battery F 161st Field Artillery

2nd Battalion 202nd Air Defense Artillery

2nd Battalion 123rd Armor
1st Battalion 131st Armor

1st Battalion 167th Cavalry
Troop E 31st Cavalry

1st Battalion 114th Aviation
Company E 245th Aviation

735th 31st 634th Support Battalion
935th Aviation Support Battalion
201st Engineer Battalion
835th Engineer Company
1009th 1310th Engineer Detachments
135th Signal Battalion
35th Military Police Company
35th Rear Operations Center
35th Material Management Center
635th Military Intelligence Battalion
135th Chemical Company

36th Infantry Division-National Guard-2004

1st Battalion 141st Infantry
3rd Battalion 141st Infantry
2nd Battalion 142nd Infantry
3rd Battalion 144th infantry

2nd Battalion 131st Field Artillery
1st Battalion 133rd Field Artillery
3rd Battalion 133rd Field Artillery
4th Battalion 133rd Field Artillery

2nd Battalion 263rd Air Defense Artillery

1st Battalion 112th Armor
2nd Battalion 112th Armor
3rd Battalion 112th Armor
4th Battalion 112th Armor
5th Battalion 112th Armor

1st Squadron 124th Cavalry
Troop G-H-I 124th Cavalry

949th 249th 536th 372nd Support Battalion
636th Aviation Support Battalion
111th 136th 386th Engineer Battalions
101st 1308th Engineer Detachments
536th Signal Battalion
236th Military Police Company
36th Rear Operations Center
36th Material Management Center
636th Military Intelligence Battalion
436th Chemical Company

38th Infantry Division-National Guard-Cyclone-2004

1st Battalion 125th Infantry
1st Battalion 148th Infantry
2nd Battalion 152nd Infantry
151st Infantry Detachment

1st Battalion 119th Field Artillery
1st Battalion 134th Field Artillery
Battery F 134th Field Artillery
Battery E 139th Field Artillery

1st Battalion 138th Air Defense Artillery

1st Battalion 126th Armor
1st Battalion 147th Armor

2nd Squadron 107th Cavalry

1st Battalion 238th Aviation
2nd Battalion 238th Aviation
Company G 238th Aviation

38th 146th 237th Support Battalions
638th Aviation Support Battalion
112th 113th Engineer Battalions
1003rd 1304th Engineer Detachments
138th Signal Battalion
38th Military Police Company

38th Material Management Center
38th Rear Operations Center
638th Military Intelligence Battalion
438th Chemical Company

40th Infantry Division-National Guard-Sunrise-2004

1st Battalion 160th Infantry
3rd Battalion 160th Infantry
1st Battalion 161st Infantry
1st Battalion 185th Infantry
160th Infantry Detachment

1st Battalion 143rd Field Artillery
1st Battalion 144th Field Artillery
2nd Battalion 146th Field Artillery
Battery D 144th Field Artillery
Battery F 144th Field Artillery

1st Battalion 188th Field Artillery

1st Battalion 149th Armor
1st Battalion 185th Armor
2nd Battalion 185th Armor
1st Battalion 303rd Armor
1st Battalion 635th Armor

1st Squadron 18th Cavalry
Troops G,H 18th Cavalry
Troop E 303rd Cavalry

1st Battalion 140th Aviation
1st Battalion 211th Aviation
Company H 140th Aviation

40th 181st 340th 540th Support Battalions
640th Aviation Support Battalion
116th 132nd 579th Engineer Battalions
1004th 1302nd Engineer Detachments
240th Signal Battalion
40th Military Police Company

40th Material Management Center
40th Rear Operations Center
640th Military Intelligence Battalion
140th Chemical Company

42nd Infantry Division-National Guard-Rainbow-2004

1st Battalion 69th Infantry
2nd Battalion 113th Infantry
1st Battalion 114th Infantry
173rd Infantry Detachment

3rd Battalion 112th Field Artillery
1st Battalion 258th Field Artillery
Battery E 101st Field Artillery
Battery D 112th Field Artillery

1st Battalion 202nd Air Defense Artillery

1st Battalion 101st Cavalry
2nd Battalion 102nd Armor
1st Battalion 127th Armor
1st Battalion 172nd Armor
2nd Battalion 172nd Armor

5th Squadron 117th Cavalry

2nd Battalion 126th Aviation
1st Battalion 142nd Aviation
Company E 126th Aviation

50th 186th 250th 342nd Support Battalions
642nd Aviation Support Battalion
101st 152nd 181st Engineer Battalions
1005th 1306th Engineer Detachments
250th Signal Battalion
42nd Military Police Company
42nd Material Management Center
42nd Rear Operations Center
642nd Military Intelligence Battalion
272nd Chemical Company

75th Division Training Support-Army Reserve-2004

1st Brigade
1st Simulation Group
2nd Simulation Group
Battle Projection Group
2nd Brigade
3rd Battalion 289th Regiment
3rd Battalion 290th Regiment
3rd Battalion 291st Regiment
1st Battalion 381st Regiment
2nd Battalion 381st Regiment
3rd Battalion 381st Regiment
2nd Battalion 382nd Regiment
1st Battalion 393rd Regiment
2nd Battalion 393rd Regiment
3rd Battalion 393rd Regiment
1st Battalion 394th Regiment
1st Battalion 395th Regiment
2nd Battalion 395th Regiment
3rd Battalion 395th Regiment
3rd Brigade
1st Battalion 291st Regiment
2nd Battalion 291st Regiment
3rd Battalion 382nd Regiment
1st Battalion 383rd Regiment
2nd Battalion 383rd Regiment
4th Brigade
1st Battalion 289th Regiment
2nd Battalion 289th Regiment
1st Battalion 290th Regiment
2nd Battalion 290th Regiment
2nd Battalion 381st Regiment
1st Battalion 382nd Regiment
3rd Battalion 383rd Regiment

78th Division Training Support-Army Reserve-Lightning-2004

1st Brigade
1st Simulation Group
2nd Simulation Group
Battle Projection Group
2nd Brigade
1st Battalion 309th Regiment
3rd Battalion 309th Regiment
2nd Battalion 310th Regiment
3rd Battalion 310th Regiment
3rd Battalion 313th Regiment
1st Battalion 314th Regiment
2nd Battalion 314th Regiment
3rd Battalion 314th Regiment
4th Brigade
1st Battalion 310th Regiment
1st Battalion 311th Regiment
2nd Battalion 311th Regiment
1st Battalion 312th Regiment
1st Battalion 313th Regiment
5th Brigade
2nd Battalion 309th Regiment
3rd Battalion 311th Regiment
2nd Battalion 312th Regiment
3rd Battalion 312th Regiment
2nd Battalion 315th Regiment
3rd Battalion 315th Regiment
1st Battalion 322nd Regiment

80th Division Institutional Training-Army Reserve Blue Ridge-2004

1st Brigade
1st Battalion 318th Regiment
2nd Battalion 318th Regiment
3rd Battalion 318th Regiment
4th Battalion 318th Regiment
2nd Brigade
1st Battalion 317th Regiment
2nd Battalion 317th Regiment
3rd Battalion 317th Regiment

1st Battalion 320th Regiment
2nd Battalion 320th Regiment
3rd Brigade
1st Battalion 80th Regiment
2nd Battalion 80th Regiment
3rd Battalion 80th Regiment
4th Battalion 80th Regiment
4th Brigade
5th Battalion 80th Regiment
6th Battalion 80th Regiment
7th Battalion 80th Regiment
Ordnance Detachment
5th Brigade
9th Battalion 80th Regiment
Practical Nurse Detachment
6th Brigade
10th Battalion 80th Regiment
11th Battalion 80th Regiment
NCOES Detachment
Drill Sgt School
7th Brigade
1st Battalion 319th Regiment
2nd Battalion 319th Regiment
3rd Battalion 319th Regiment
ROTC Brigade

82 Airborne Division-Active Component-All American-2004

1st Battalion 325th Infantry
2nd Battalion 325th Infantry
3rd Battalion 325th Infantry
1st Battalion 504th Infantry
2nd Battalion 504th Infantry
3rd Battalion 504th Infantry
1st Battalion 505th Infantry
2nd Battalion 505th Infantry
3rd Battalion 505th Infantry

1st Battalion 319th Field Artillery
2nd Battalion 319th Field Artillery
3rd Battalion 319th Field Artillery

1st Field Artillery Detachment

3rd Battalion 4th Air Defense Artillery

1st Squadron 17th Cavalry

1st Battalion 82nd Aviation
2nd Battalion 82nd Aviation
Company B 1st Battalion 58th Aviation

782nd 82nd 307th 407th Support Battalions
307th Engineer Battalion
82nd Signal Battalion
82nd Military Police Company
182nd Material Management Center
82nd Rear Operations Center
313th Military Intelligence Battalion
21st Chemical Company

84th Division Institutional Training-Army Reserve-Ralspitters-2004

1st Brigade
1st Battalion 329th Regiment
2nd Battalion 329th Regiment
1st Battalion 330th Regiment
2nd Battalion 330th Regiment
1st Battalion 333rd Regiment
2nd Battalion 333rd Regiment
2nd Brigade
1st Battalion 274th Regiment
2nd Battalion 274th Regiment
3rd Battalion 274th Regiment
2nd Battalion 334th Regiment
3rd Battalion 334th Regiment
2nd Battalion 339th Regiment
3rd Brigade
1st Battalion 84th Regiment
2nd Battalion 84th Regiment
3rd Battalion 84th Regiment
4th Battalion 84th Regiment
5th Battalion 84th Regiment

6th Battalion 84th Regiment
4th Brigade
7th Battalion 84th Regiment
8th Battalion 84th Regiment
9th Battalion 84th Regiment
10th Battalion 84th Regiment
Ordnance Detachment
5th Brigade
11th Battalion 84th Regiment
Practical Nurse Detachment
6th Brigade
12th Battalion 84th Regiment
13th Battalion 84th Regiment
14th Battalion 84th Regiment
NCOES Detachment
Drill Sgt School
7th Brigade
1st Battalion 334th Regiment
2nd Battalion 339th Regiment
3rd Battalion 339th Regiment
ROTC Brigade

85th Division Institutional Training-Army Reserve-Custer-2004

1st Brigade
1st Simulation Group
2nd simulation Group
Battle Projection Group
2nd Brigade
3rd Battalion 335th Regiment
1st Battalion 338th Regiment
1st Battalion 340th Regiment
2nd Battalion 411th Regiment
3rd Brigade
1st Battalion 335th Regiment
2nd Battalion 335th Regiment
2nd Battalion 337th Regiment
2nd Battalion 338th Regiment
3rd Battalion 338th Regiment
3rd Battalion 411th Regiment
4th Brigade

1st Battalion 337th Regiment
3rd Battalion 337th Regiment
2nd Battalion 340th Regiment
1st Battalion 409th Regiment
2nd Battalion 409th Regiment
3rd Battalion 409th Regiment
1st Battalion 410th Regiment
2nd Battalion 410th Regiment
3rd Battalion 410th Regiment
1st Battalion 411th Regiment

87th Division Training Support-Army Reserve-Acorn-2004

1st Brigade
1st Simulation Group
2nd Simulation Group
Battle Projection Group
2nd Brigade
3rd Battalion 347th Regiment
2nd Battalion 348th Regiment
3rd Battalion 348th Regiment
1st Battalion 350th Regiment
2nd Battalion 350th Regiment
2nd Battalion 351st Regiment
3rd Battalion 351st Regiment
3rd Brigade
1st Battalion 305th Regiment
2nd Battalion 305th Regiment
3rd Battalion 305th Regiment
1st Battalion 346th Regiment
2nd Battalion 346th Regiment
3rd Battalion 346th Regiment
3rd Battalion 349th Regiment
4th Brigade
1st Battalion 306th Regiment
2nd Battalion 306th Regiment
3rd Battalion 306th Regiment
1st Battalion 347th Regiment
2nd Battalion 349th Regiment
1st Battalion 351st Regiment
5th Brigade

1st Battalion 307th Regiment
2nd Battalion 307th Regiment
3rd Battalion 307th Regiment
1st Battalion 345th Regiment
2nd Battalion 345th Regiment
2nd Battalion 347th Regiment
1st Battalion 349th Regiment

91st Division Training Support-Army Reserve-Powder River-2004

1st Brigade
1st Simulation Group
2nd Simulation Group
3rd Simulation Group
Battle Projection Group
2nd Brigade
2nd Battalion 356th Regiment
1st Battalion 359th Regiment
1st Battalion 360th Regiment
2nd Battalion 360th Regiment
3rd Battalion 360th Regiment
1st Battalion 361st Regiment
2nd Battalion 361st Regiment
3rd Battalion 361st Regiment
1st Battalion 362nd Regiment
2nd Battalion 362nd Regiment
3rd Battalion 362nd Regiment
3rd Brigade
3rd Battalion 356th Regiment
1st Battalion 363rd Regiment
2nd Battalion 363rd Regiment
3rd Battalion 363rd Regiment
4th Brigade
1st Battalion 356th Regiment
1st Battalion 357th Regiment
2nd Battalion 357th Regiment
3rd Battalion 357th Regiment
1st Battalion 358th Regiment
2nd Battalion 358th Regiment
3rd Battalion 358th Regiment
1st Battalion 364th Regiment

2nd Battalion 364th Regiment
3rd Battalion 364th Regiment

95th Division Institutional Training-Army Reserve-Iron Men of Metz-2004

1st Brigade
1st Battalion 354th Regiment
2nd Battalion 354th Regiment
3rd Battalion 354th Regiment
1st Battalion 355th Regiment
2nd Battalion 355th Regiment
2nd Brigade
1st Battalion 377th Regiment
2nd Battalion 377th Regiment
3rd Battalion 377th Regiment
1st Battalion 378th Regiment
2nd Battalion 378th Regiment
3rd Battalion 378th Regiment
3rd Brigade
1st Battalion 95th Regiment
2nd Battalion 95th Regiment
3rd Battalion 95th Regiment
4th Battalion 95th Regiment
5th Battalion 95th Regiment
6th Battalion 95th Regiment
4th Brigade
7th Battalion 95th Regiment
8th Battalion 95th Regiment
9th Battalion 95th Regiment
Regional Training Site (Maintenance)
Ordnance Detachment
5th Brigade
10th Battalion 95th Regiment
Practical Nurse Detachment
3457th Medical Training Center
6th Brigade
11th Battalion 95th Regiment
12th Battalion 95th Regiment
9052nd 9053rd Training Detachments
NCOES Detachment
Drill Sgt School

7th Brigade
1st Battalion 379th Regiment
2nd Battalion 379th Regiment
3rd Battalion 379th Regiment
ROTC Brigade

98th Division Institutional Training-Army Reserve-Iroquois-2004

1st Brigade
1st Battalion 304th Regiment
2nd Battalion 304th Regiment
1st Battalion 385th Regiment
2nd Battalion 385th Regiment
1st Battalion 417th Regiment
2nd Battalion 417th Regiment
3rd Battalion 417th Regiment
2nd Brigade
1st Battalion 389th Regiment
2nd Battalion 389th Regiment
3rd Battalion 389th Regiment
1st Battalion 390th Regiment
2nd Battalion 390th Regiment
3rd Battalion 390th Regiment
3rd Brigade
1st Battalion 98th Regiment
2nd Battalion 98th Regiment
3rd Battalion 98th Regiment
4th Battalion 98th Regiment
5th Battalion 98th Regiment
6th Battalion 98th Regiment
4th Brigade
7th Battalion 98th Regiment
8th Battalion 98th Regiment
9th Battalion 98th Regiment
10th Battalion 98th Regiment
Ordnance Detachment
5th Brigade
11th Battalion 98th Regiment
Practical Nurse Detachment
6th Brigade
12th Battalion 98th Regiment

13th Battalion 98th Regiment
14th Battalion 98th Regiment
NCOES Detachment
Drill Sgt School
7th Brigade
3rd Battalion 304th Regiment
1st Battalion 391st Regiment
2nd Battalion 391st Regiment
3rd Battalion 391st Regiment
ROTC Brigade

100th Division Institutional Training-Army Reserve-Century-2004

1st Brigade
1st Battalion 397th Regiment
2nd Squadron 397th Cavalry
3rd Squadron 397th Cavalry
2nd Brigade
1st Battalion 398th Regiment
3rd Battalion 398th Regiment
3rd Battalion 399th Regiment
3rd Brigade
1st Battalion 100th Regiment
2nd Battalion 100th Regiment
3rd Battalion 100th Regiment
4th Battalion 100th Regiment
4th Brigade
5th Battalion 100th Regiment
6th Battalion 100th Regiment
7th Battalion 100th Regiment
4th Battalion 398th Regiment
Ordnance Detachment
5th Brigade
8th Battalion 100th Regiment
Practical Nurse Detachment
6th Brigade
9th Battalion 100th Regiment
10th Battalion 100th Regiment
NCOES Detachment
Drill Sgt School
7th Brigade
1st Battalion 399th Regiment

2nd Battalion 399th Regiment
ROTC Brigade
4th Battalion 399th Regiment

101st Airborne Division-Active Component-Screaming Eagles-2004

1st Brigade Unit of Action
1st Battalion 327th Infantry
2nd Battalion 327th Infantry
2nd Squadron 61st Cavalry
2nd Battalion 320th Field Artillery
426th Forward Support Battalion
1st Brigade Troop Battalion

2nd Brigade Unit of Action
1st Battalion 502nd Infantry
2nd Battalion 502nd Infantry
1st Squadron 75th Cavalry
1st Battalion 320th Field Artillery
526th Forward Support Battalion
2nd Brigade Troop Battalion

3rd Brigade Unit of Action
1st Battalion 187th Infantry
2nd Battalion 187th Infantry
2nd Squadron 75th Cavalry
3rd Battalion 320th Field Artillery
626th Forward Support Battalion
3rd Brigade Troop Battalion

4th Brigade Unit of Action
3rd Battalion 187th Infantry
3rd Battalion 327th Infantry
1st Squadron 61st Cavalry
4th Battalion 320th Field Artillery
801st Forward Support Battalion
4th Brigade Troop Battalion

101st Aviation Brigade
1st Battalion 101st Aviation
2nd Battalion 101st Aviation

5th Battalion 101st Aviation
6th Battalion 101st Aviation
2nd Squadron 17th Cavalry
96th Aviation Support Battalion

159th Aviation Brigade
3rd Battalion 101st Aviation
4th Battalion 101st Aviation
7th Battalion 101st Aviation
9th Battalion 101st Aviation
1st Squadron 17th Cavalry
563rd Aviation Support Battalion

Division Support Brigade
129th Corps Support Battalion
561st Corps Support Battalion
106th Transportation Battalion
101st Soldier Support Battalion

Special Support Battalion

104th Division Institutional Training-Timerwolves-2004

1st Brigade
1st Battalion 413th Regiment
1st Battalion 414th Regiment
2nd Battalion 414th Regiment
1st Battalion 415th Regiment
2nd Battalion 415th Regiment
3rd Battalion 415th Regiment
1043rd Detachment CDDS
3rd Brigade
1st Battalion 104th Regiment
2nd Battalion 104th Regiment
3rd Battalion 104th Regiment
4th Battalion 104th Regiment
5th Battalion 104th Regiment
1041st Detachment
SC Detachment
4960th Multi-Functional Training Brigade
1st Battalion

2nd Battalion

2nd Battalion
3rd Battalion
4th Brigade
6th Battalion 104th Regiment
7th Battalion 104th Regiment
8th Battalion 104th Regiment
1042nd Ordnance Detachment
5th Brigade
9th Battalion 104th Regiment
Practical Nurse Detachment
6th Brigade
10th Battalion 104th Regiment
11th Battalion 104th Regiment
12th Battalion 104th Regiment
NOCES Detachment
Drill Sgt School
7th Brigade
1st Battalion 413th Regiment
3rd Battalion 413th Regiment
ROTC Brigade
3rd Battalion 414th Regiment

108th Division Institutional Training-Army Reserve-Golden Griffon-2004

1st Brigade
1st Battalion 321st Regiment
3rd Battalion 323rd Regiment
2nd Battalion 485th Regiment
1st Battalion 518th Regiment
2nd Brigade
2nd Battalion 321st Regiment
1st Battalion 323rd Regiment
3rd Battalion 323rd Regiment
1st Battalion 485th Regiment
3rd Battalion 518th Regiment
3rd Brigade
1st Battalion 108th Regiment
2nd Battalion 108th Regiment
3rd Battalion 108th Regiment
4th Battalion 108th Regiment
5th Battalion 108th Regiment

6th Battalion 108th Regiment
4th Brigade
7th Battalion 108th Regiment
8th Battalion 108th Regiment
9th Battalion 108th Regiment
Ordnance Detachment
5th Brigade
10th Battalion 108th Regiment
Practical Nurse Detachment
6th Brigade
11th Battalion 108th Regiment
12th Battalion 108th Regiment
NCOES Detachment
Drill Sgt School
7th Brigade
3rd Battalion 321st Regiment
2nd Battalion 518th Regiment
8th Brigade
1st Combat Support Battalion
2nd Combat Service Battalion
3rd Health Services Battalion
4th Professional Development Battalion
ROTC Brigade

79th "Lorraine" Division

From the division's service in France, World War I

84th Infantry Division

The logo invokes President Abraham Lincoln. The division originated in Illinois, where the President's had worked as a rail-splitter.

www.ingramcontent.com/pod-product-compliance
Lightning Source LLC
Chambersburg PA
CBHW062041090426
42740CB00016B/2977

9 780972 029650